The **ScotWays** Guide to the
Law of Access to Land in Scotland

The **ScotWays** Guide to the Law of Access to Land in Scotland

Malcolm M. Combe

JOHN DONALD

with

First published in Great Britain in 2018 by
John Donald, an imprint of Birlinn Ltd

West Newington House
10 Newington Road
Edinburgh
EH9 1QS

www.birlinn.co.uk

ISBN: 978 1 910900 28 4

British Library Cataloguing-in-Publication Data
A catalogue record for this book is available
on request from the British Library

Typeset by Mark Blackadder

Printed and bound in Britain by
Bell and Bain Ltd, Glasgow

Contents

Foreword

Scotland has unique and progressive rights of access to land for the public. Naturally, these rights are defined and this guide provides a detailed explanation. ScotWays has published guides before, the last in 2006, but the law moves on and this new version, published 15 years after the Land Reform (Scotland) Act 2003, states our view of it as at the end of July 2018.

This new guide is intended for members of the public, landowners and managers, access professionals and legal advisers.

ScotWays is exceptionally grateful to Malcolm Combe, a senior lecturer in law at the University of Aberdeen, who has provided a detailed yet lucid explanation of the law. Malcolm is well known for his expertise in this area and commentary on the subject. He readily agreed to undertake this huge task and did so with great good humour and to a demanding time schedule. He has donated his fee to Friends of ANCHOR, a charity that supports cancer and haematology patients in the north east of Scotland. He came to rely on them (and too many others to mention) when faced with a challenge to his health.

We are grateful to ScotWays director, John Elliot, who ably led this project on behalf of the Board. We are also grateful to others who have contributed, including Judith Lewis, who compiled the index and provided valuable help with the production process, Richard Barron, who made detailed and insightful comments, and Douglas Cusine, who reviewed the text.

We are very appreciative of the financial support for the publication from the Scottish Mountaineering Council Trust and from the Geraldine Kirkpatrick Charitable Trust.

Muriel Robertson
Chair, The Scottish Rights of Way and Access Society (ScotWays).

Abbreviations

Access Code or Code	Scottish Outdoor Access Code
access authority	Local authority or national park authority, as applicable
asp	Act of the Scottish Parliament
ScotWays	The Scottish Rights of Way and Access Society
SNH	Scottish Natural Heritage
1967 Act	Countryside (Scotland) Act 1967
1973 Act	Prescription and Limitation (Scotland) Act 1973
1984 Act	Roads (Scotland) Act 1984
1994 Act	Criminal Justice and Public Order Act 1994
1997 Act	Town and Country Planning (Scotland) Act 1997
2003 Act	Land Reform (Scotland) Act 2003 (asp 2)
2016 Act	Land Reform (Scotland) Act 2016 (asp 18)

Introduction, Structure and Content

This book is a journey. It is a journey through Scotland, Highland and Lowland, urban and rural. It will take you across glens and up bens, through straths, cleughs, neuks and underpasses. It might even navigate you along a river or canal, or accompany you as dip your toes in a loch or lochan, stop in a corrie for a picnic, or investigate a historic broch or geological feature.

It will do all these things, but only up to a point. This is not a guidebook in the usual sense of the term. It will not, for example, tell you the most scenic or energy-efficient route up a Munro, Corbett, Donald or Graham, or indeed highlight the best spot to park a vehicle in order to access one of Scotland's many beautiful vistas.

Except, in a way, it will. It will explain how the law of the land works to regulate access to Scotland's outdoors. It will look at who might be entitled to access land or inland waters, who (if anyone) can set the agenda about whether or how access can be taken to any given spot, and the activities people are entitled to do there. It will even consider whether, and if so where, you can park before setting off on foot, bicycle or by any other means to enjoy the outdoors.

Every legal system that recognises private ownership of land has rules governing the apparently simple yet potentially multi-layered activity of taking access. Scots law is such a legal system. For many years there has been a certain tradition of access across Scotland, which has recently been augmented by a modern statutory regime. An understanding of these multi-layered rules is crucial, to allow everyone to know the extent of their rights and responsibilities and, in turn, to minimise and resolve conflict.

Even with the best will in the world, conflict can occur. Differing perspectives about access can lead to disputes, and taking access to land for passage or other activities can be both a practical and an emotive issue.

For landowners, land managers or any other occupiers, there might be a fear of irresponsible land access causing damage to property (including the land itself or any moveable items on it) or wildlife, not to mention the simple fact that access takers could obstruct a legitimate land use. There might also be issues that are more difficult to quantify, such as concerns about privacy or safety.

By contrast, members of the public might wish to get from A to B in a simple and non-intrusive way. For those who do not have a particular destination in mind, or who wish to enjoy access at their leisure, there may be historical, cultural or even health-related reasons why people feel that access to land not owned by them is important. Being denied access to large swathes of the outdoors for recreation or to learn about wildlife could have quite an impact on a significant number of people. Whilst recognising legitimate concerns about irresponsible or selfish access by some, responsible access takers might baulk at being lumped together with such individuals, especially if they are willing and able to conduct themselves in a way that will not interfere with a landowner's chosen activity.

A balance must be struck. In Scotland, public rights of way might allow people to travel from one public place to another (often along traditional routes to, for example, a market, kirk or cemetery), with no need to ask a landowner's permission. These rights continue in the modern era, but the most important law for many access takers is now the Land Reform (Scotland) Act 2003. Part 1 of the 2003 Act liberalised access to Scotland's outdoors by allowing recreational, educational and, in some cases, commercial access to be taken over land, with an additional right to cross land (separate to existing rights of way), without the landowner's prior consent. That sounds striking, but the 2003 Act does not establish a free-for-all. These rights are subject to two important qualifications: (a) the land must not be excluded from the scope of the 2003 Act, owing perhaps to the characteristics of the land; and (b) any access taken must be responsible. Even with those qualifications, the potential coverage of the law is vast, and it is simply not possible to understand the law on outdoor access without understanding its terms.

Structure and content

This book aims to provide a user-friendly guide to the law, with particular reference to public rights of way and the right of responsible access.

After this Introduction, the next chapter will give an overview of the current legal framework and briefly explain how public access rights contrast to private rights of access, before explaining how public rights of way or other rights of public access co-exist with the newer right of responsible access. Reference will also be made to the public's traditional right of access to the foreshore and navigable rivers.

Chapter 2 will consider the right of responsible access, which is sometimes referred to as 'the right to roam'. Given the potential scope of activities covered this forms a first port of call for many outdoor access questions.

Chapter 3 considers public rights of way, explaining their continuing relevance and making particular reference to situations where a right of access might be referable only to a public right of way because the right of responsible access does not apply.

Chapters 4 and 5 draw some conclusions and explain what the public can do in relation to access issues as a whole, with reference to the role of access authorities and court processes.

Three appendices set out: (1) a process for establishing a public right of way; (2) an introduction to the Scottish Outdoor Access Code, which is influential in determining what is responsible access and responsible land management; and (3) questions to determine whether access is permissible. Tables of statutes, of cases and an index follow.

This guide has two audiences in mind. The first is the general public. A key aim of this guide is for it to be an accessible book about access for a reader who is broadly interested in the subject or for someone who is seeking an outline answer to a specific point.

The other audience is the more specialised readership that might be described as 'access practitioners' who will demand more background, detail and references than others to allow issues to be fully explored or, where that is not possible in this guide, further research to be undertaken.

Rather than be split into two completely different sections, which would inevitably lead to duplication within this guide and might even lead to information being missed by a reader, it is structured in a way to provide maximum benefit to those two audiences. Topics within each chapter will be separated into segments with relevant subheadings, and each of these segments will normally be presented with initial content followed by detailed content. The initial content will be thorough but targeted, with only a bare minimum of referencing. The more detailed content will provide further analysis, together with statutory references, case law citations to reported judgments, and other relevant material. The more detailed text is clearly identified by indentation and smaller text size, and always appears under a heading with the words 'Additional information' at the end. Where no section labelled 'Additional information' is given, this means further elaboration is unnecessary.

This approach means there will be no need to leaf from one section of the book to another for any given aspect of the law. It will also allow a non-specialist reader to have easy access to more information for a specific question or indeed where interest has been piqued for any given topic. Notes and references are gathered together at the end of the book under the relevant chapter headings.

With that route map in place, our journey through Scots law begins.

Updates

Please note that updates to this text will be available from the Scot-Ways website (www.scotways.com).

1
Overview of the Current Legal Framework

This chapter briefly explains the rules by which access to land can be taken in Scotland, with particular reference to the two most important sets of rules: a) public rights of way; and b) the right of responsible access that was introduced by the Land Reform (Scotland) Act 2003. Some comment is offered on how these rules interact, whilst other ways access to land can be taken will be highlighted.

In this chapter, as in the other chapters of this guide, there are two levels of text. Standard text presents the overall situation, then more detailed text follows under headings marked 'Additional information' and identified by indentation and a smaller text size.

Background to the current legal framework
for public access to land

A landowner has various entitlements. An important entitlement is the right to use land, such as by walking across or around it, or engaging in some other activity on it. This much is well understood by lawyers and non-lawyers alike. If this guide was restricted to the topic of taking access to land that you own, it could have been much shorter than it is. The more pressing issue is whether you can take access over someone else's land. In many circumstances you can, and you can even do so without prior permission from the landowner. Conversely, other people might be able to take access over land you own. How can this be?

Until 2005, public rights of way were the main form of legally protected access in Scotland. There are many rights of way throughout the country. Some of these have a long history and may have been used, for example, as drove roads, or served as the only way of travelling between isolated communities. Some rights of way are well documented and signposted, but others are unrecorded and known only to the local people who use them. The core of the regulatory regime for these public rights of way flows from something called the common law. This means that rights of way were not specifically designed by the UK Parliament at Westminster or the Scottish Parliament at Holyrood, or indeed the old Scottish Parliament that existed before the Act of Union which joined Scotland and England and Wales as the United Kingdom. Instead, the rules flow from traditional sources and are interpreted by our law courts, although some parliamentary reforms of the common law have taken place.

As we shall see, a member of the public is generally able to traverse all or part of a public right of way without fear of interruption by the landowner (or landowners) of the ground in question, or indeed anyone else, assuming that access is being taken by way of a suitable mode of transport for that route. Public rights of way are not the full story though. There are also traditional rights of access to the foreshore (that is to say, the coastal area between the high and low tide marks) and navigable rivers. There is then the simple fact that many landowners in Scotland have traditionally tolerated access to the countryside over their land, particularly in upland areas. Over the years, statutory powers have also been introduced for some public authorities to create 'public paths' (although, as we shall see, these powers are not so important in the present day). This means that access takers have often not been restricted to using rights of way.

In 2003, the Scottish Parliament passed an important statute which shifted the focus even further away from public rights of way. The Land Reform (Scotland) Act 2003 (referred to in this guide as 'the 2003 Act') granted much more extensive public access rights to land. Its opening section provides that 'everyone' has the statutory rights established by Part 1 of the Act, as explained in detail below. The provisions of the 2003 Act which relate to public access to land came into force on 9 February 2005. Operating together with public rights of way, these statutory rights have considerably enhanced the general public's access to Scotland's land and inland waters. They apply across much of Scotland's outdoors, including a network of core paths, which were also provided for by the 2003 Act. As we shall see, these core paths are not necessarily public rights of way, but they do provide demarcated routes where people can be confident that the right of responsible access will apply.

Even with the 2003 Act and other rights of access, there may be situations where there is no applicable access regime. In those situations, and where there is no consent from the relevant landowner, then the common law of trespass remains to be applied. It is sometimes said that there is no law of trespass in Scotland. As we shall see in this guide, that is not quite the whole story.

Background to the current legal framework for public access to land – Additional information

There are various sources of Scots law. In addition to laws made in Parliament (whether by Westminster, Holyrood, or the old Scottish parliament), there are important 'Institutional writers', such as Erskine and Bell, whose writings can still be an authoritative source of Scots law. No statute sets out the rights of a landowner in detail, which means that other sources must be looked at to ascertain these. Both Erskine[1] and Bell[2] explain that proprietors start from a position that gives exclusive use of land that they own.

In terms of what this means for a properly advised and vigilant landowner, she can take steps to prevent a crane jib swinging over her property[3] or take similar legal steps in relation to a drone flying over her property. Encroachments by way of building can be prevented or (should it be too late to prevent such intrusion) removed.[4] Steps can also be taken against wandering animate objects: straying animals can be removed and damage caused by them is attributed to the keeper of those animals under the Animals (Scotland) Act 1987. The rules about straying humans will be analysed in the course of this guide.

For policy and practical reasons, the law chips away at the idea that a landowner can absolutely exclude others from her land in various ways. Part 1 of the Land Reform (Scotland) Act 2003 (asp 2) is one recent example of this.[5] Public rights of way are a more traditional exception.

As noted, there are other ways access can be taken. The rights in relation to the foreshore and navigable rivers are geographically specific. Nothing more is said of them at this stage, but it is important to be aware of them. Reference should also be made to the Countryside (Scotland) Act 1967 Act. Part 3 of this legislation introduced provision for 'public paths'. Although open to the public, such paths were not true public rights of way and could not be enforced directly by members of the public. This legislation has largely been superseded by the 2003 Act, although it does remain in force for certain purposes. It can also be noted in passing that it is acceptable to take access to another person's land of necessity, to escape a peril or to intervene to avert a dangerous situation.[6]

The thorny issue of trespass is one that will be returned to in some detail below. For present purposes, it can be acknowledged that a custom of tolerance and the practicalities relating to obtaining an interdict (a court order preventing a named person from doing something) have contributed to the perception that there is no law of trespass in Scotland, but the balance of scholarly authority tends towards the position that the underlying law of Scotland allows a landowner to exert a significant amount of control over access to her land.[7]

The modern access regime: features and personalities

An important innovation provided for by the 2003 Act is the Scottish Outdoor Access Code. This document, which was drafted by Scottish Natural Heritage and approved by a vote in the Scottish Parliament, facilitates access and understanding of access law. It is available at www.outdooraccess-scotland.com. It will be explained more fully below. Its focus is on the right of responsible access. Access takers must exercise rights of access responsibly, and owners of land have a reciprocal duty to look after their land in a way that respects those rights of access. When an access taker is not complying with the Code, that is a strong indicator that access is not being taken responsibly. An almost mirror provision operates to provide that when landowners (or other occupiers of land) do not have regard to the guidance on responsible conduct set out in the Code that will be an indicator they are not acting responsibly.

Despite that focus on responsible access, the Access Code also contains information about (for example) public rights of way and specific criminal offences that access takers should be aware of. It is an important resource and this guide does not seek to replace it, but the Code is *not* a definitive statement of the law. (Neither is this guide a definitive statement of the law, although it does seek to provide a level of detail about the overall regime for accessing land in Scotland that the Code does not provide.) It should also be stressed that the central importance of the Code relates to the issue of what makes responsible access or responsible conduct, and as such it is not definitive when it comes to legal questions about (for example) whether land is excluded from the scope of access rights.

Whilst the legwork of preparing the Access Code was a large part of Scottish Natural Heritage's role, SNH continues to have a role in publicising the Code and promoting an understanding of it. Further, the Code is not designed to stand still. SNH has a continuing duty to keep the Code under review and may modify it from time to time.

Scotland's 32 local authorities and, where relevant, two national park authorities have a role in relation to access rights in their respective areas. They have certain roles in relation to public rights of way, but they have particular roles and powers in the 2003 Act when it comes to upholding and enforcing access rights. They also played a central role in preparing core path plans when core paths were introduced and have a continuing role in relation to the amendment of these plans.

The 2003 Act provides that in each access region a local access forum will operate. These representative bodies play a consultative role and work with access authorities to advise and, if appropriate, give assistance about access issues local to them.

Community councils are local representative bodies in Scotland that play a part in, for example, the planning process. They have only one role in relation to the 2003 Act, namely as a consultee during the preparation of access byelaws. They may also play an important informal role in improving communication between members of the public and planning authorities, which may be especially relevant when dealing with public rights of way.

Other non-statutory bodies in Scotland, such as the Ramblers Association and indeed ScotWays, take an interest in access matters. Important as these bodies are, it is local authorities or national parks as access authorities supported by local access forums that have a specific role in terms of the day-to-day operation of the 2003 Act.

None of this should be taken as meaning that private individuals have no role to play. They can – and do – play a part in ensuring appropriate access takes place in Scotland. This role can involve making representations to the personalities already mentioned, but it may extend to taking matters to court in certain circumstances.

The modern access regime: features and personalities – Additional information

Scottish Natural Heritage is a statutory body.[8] Having fulfilled its duty of preparing the Scottish Outdoor Access Code (under section 10 of the 2003 Act), SNH plays less of a role in day-to-day access matters, although it has powers to protect the natural heritage of land in respect of which access rights are exercisable (under section 29 of the 2003 Act). SNH's role in relation to the Code is to publicise it (a duty shared with access authorities) and to promote under-standing of it.[9] It also has a duty to keep the Code under review:[10] SNH encourages correspondence about any issues with the Code.[11] As and when it reviews the Code, SNH is mandated to consult with such persons and bodies as they think appropriate.

The Access Code will be discussed more fully below. For present purposes, it can be highlighted that section 2(2)(b)(i) of the 2003 Act provides that in the calculation of whether an access taker (or purported access taker) is responsible, regard is to be had as to whether that person has disregarded the guidance in the Code. It also has an important and wide role in determining what is respon-sible land management, as demonstrated in the case of *Renyana Stahl Anstalt* v *Loch Lomond and the Trossachs National Park Auth-ority*.[12] As for the status of the Code in relation to other matters, observations in a Sheriff Court case suggest that it is of limited use when determining whether land is excluded,[13] although another case in the Sheriff Appeal Court has approved a passage of it.[14] All of this will be discussed further below.

The role of local authorities[15] and national parks[16] as access champions is mandated in the 2003 Act, Part 1, Chapter 5. Particular roles will be identified over the course of this guide, over and above the already highlighted roles in relation to the duty to uphold access rights (section 13) and core paths (sections 17–20D). The provisions on the interaction of local authorities and local access forums are found in section 25 of the 2003 Act. Section 32 of the 2003 Act defines 'local authority' as meaning the relevant national park or council for the area where the land in respect of which access rights are exercisable is located. In this guide, 'access authority' will be used as the composite term where appropriate. In 2005, the Scottish Executive (as the Scottish Government was then known) published its Guidance for Local Authorities and National Park Authorities (available at www.gov.scot/Publications/2005/02/20645/51835). This was revised in January 2014 to take into account reforms relating to the closure of core paths. It has not yet been revised to take into account the changes in Part 9 of the 2016 Act. Those changes are relatively minor, although the new rules for the amendment of core paths plans will need particular consideration by access authorities.

As regards a local authority's role relating to public rights of way, section 23 of the 2003 Act (which relates to the reinstatement of ploughed land) applies to both core paths that can be used for responsible access and public rights of way. Then there are some specific statutory rules for public rights of way only (such as section 46 of the Countryside (Scotland) Act 1967, which mandates the protection and maintenance of rights of way).

Relationship of statutory access rights and rights of way

Despite the wide application of the statutory rights of access afforded to everyone in terms of the 2003 Act, rights of way continue to be relevant. The right of responsible access does not diminish or displace public rights of way, and any existing legal rights at common law such as servitudes (which are explained immediately below) or public rights of way will not be extinguished or replaced. However, those seeking access may wish to exercise their statutory rights rather than rely on any vagueness of the common law, especially in a situation where the scope of a servitude or a public right of way is unclear. This might be the case when a servitude or public right of way has been constituted by long-term usage by a legal device called positive prescription. Positive prescription allows an entitlement to be established by making use of land as of right (that is to say, with impunity as if the right already exists) for at least 20 years. In that situation, as shall be seen below, the extent of the usage in the prescriptive period will then dictate the extent of the right that is established, but this might not be clear to all parties whereas the scope of statutory access rights will be comparatively easy to ascertain.

That leads on to a strange irony, namely that the existence of the new statutory access rights may make it difficult to establish a new public right of way. This is because it is provided in the 2003 Act that the exercise of statutory access rights does not, of itself, amount to the exercise of possession needed for a new right of way to be constituted. In other words, use of the statutory access rights will not normally count towards use of a route for the 20-year period necessary to create a right of way by the process of positive prescription.

Public rights of way continue to be important though and may exist over land where the statutory rights of access do not and cannot apply, such as a path close to a house or a field where crops are growing. Where the public rights created in the 2003 Act do not apply, a person wishing to cross land may still do so if a public right of way exists.

It can also be noted that there is some overlap to the governing regime for public rights of way and the new statutory rights of access despite the various legal distinctions between them. Certain of the statutory provisions in the 2003 Act are applied equally to them, relative to: a) prohibition of signs, obstructions and dangerous impediments; and b) the local authority's powers in respect of measures for safety, protection and guidance and assistance. So too do relevant provisions of the criminal law generally apply equally to public rights of way and statutory access rights.

Relationship of statutory access rights and rights of way – Additional information

The 2003 Act makes a number of important declarations on the interaction of access rights and rights of way. Section 5(3) provides that the newer rights have no negative impact on other rights:

> The existence or exercise of access rights does not diminish or displace any other rights (whether public or private) of entry, way, passage or access.

Section 5(5) then states access rights cannot be used to constitute new rights. It provides:

> The exercise of access rights does not of itself amount to the exercise or possession of any right for the purpose of any enactment or rule of law relating to the circumstances in which a right of way or servitude or right of public navigation may be constituted.

This has an impact on the process of positive prescription. Positive prescription is a legal method whereby public rights of way can be created by the exercise of a route as of right for 20 years, in terms of the Prescription and Limitation (Scotland) Act 1973. The process will be explained further below when dealing with the creation of rights of way, but for present purposes it can be noted that section 5(5) of the 2003 Act means no access attributable to the right of responsible access can be counted towards the 20 years required for positive prescription. It can be noted that the wording of this provision, with its focus on routes that 'may be constituted', only applies in relation to the creation of new rights of way. This section does not affect existing rights of way.

The exemplar exclusions from the scope of access rights (a path near a home and land where crops have been sown or are growing) are provided for in section 6(1)(b)(iv) and section 6(1)(i) respectively. They and other exclusions are discussed further below. The importance of rights of way in such circumstances can be demonstrated by the case of *Fife Council* v *Nisbet*,[17] a situation where the proximity of the land to the house meant the new access regime was not an appropriate means by which to combat an access restriction.

Overlap between public rights of way and statutory access rights is specifically provided for by section 31 of the 2003 Act, applying the rules about discouraging, blocking or hindering access[18] and providing for measures relating to safety, protection, guidance and assistance[19] across both regimes.

Public and private rights of access

This guide is concerned with public rights of way in Scotland and the new statutory rights of access to land. As such, this guide does not deal with 'private' or 'servitude' rights of way. Servitudes of access may be created by agreement between adjacent landowners or by some other means and are enforceable only by the owner of land that benefits from the servitude. They are roughly equivalent to rights known as 'easements' elsewhere in the United Kingdom and in the Irish Republic.

A public right of way benefits members of the public generally and may be enforceable by members of the public whether or not the individual wishing to enforce the public right of way owns any land. This is equally so in relation to the statutory rights conferred by the 2003 Act. It is of course possible that a member of the public may wish to use a public right of way or the statutory right to cross land created by the 2003 Act in order to gain access to his own land, but that does not convert the public right of way or the statutory right into a servitude of access.

Public and private rights of access – Additional information

Servitudes can be of crucial domestic or commercial importance, but they are not an appropriate means by which the world at large can take access to someone's land. Further reading on the topic can be found in Cusine and Paisley, *Servitudes and Rights of Way*.[20]

The occasional similarity and overlap of servitudes and rights of way cannot be denied though. It is evidenced by the title and coverage of the book just referred to, and also by the above mentioned section 5(3) of the 2003 Act, which makes clear that private rights of access are not affected by the right of responsible access.

On the issue of 'private' or 'servitude' rights of way, see *Thomson v Murdoch*.[21] A public right of way and a servitude right of access may co-exist in relation to the same burdened land.[22]

As noted, agreement is one of the ways in which servitudes may be created, but there are various other means, principally exercise as of right for 20 years. There is some similarity here between constitution of a servitude and constitution of public right of way by exercise as of right for 20 years, and indeed this matter is covered in the same section of the Prescription and Limitation (Scotland) Act 1973 (section 3). It can however be noted that a public right of way must have public termini at both ends. This means that a servitude might be constituted by taking access from a private place over adjacent land, whereas a public right of way could not be so constituted.

Ownership of underlying ground

The ownership of the track, path or road which a public right of way may follow remains with the owner of the ground. Similarly, the ownership of land affected by statutory access rights remains with the landowner. As a result, the ownership of anything growing there such as flowers, shrubs or grass remains with the owner of the land. Consequently, a person using a public right of way has no entitlement to pick wild flowers just because she is exercising a public right of way. So too a person using a public right of way or statutory access rights is not entitled to damage the underlying ground by means such as depositing rubbish or dumping chemicals, or acting as if she were the owner by carrying out activity such as digging up the soil, installing drains or laying cables. Furthermore, people exercising their statutory rights of access must do so responsibly. This means they must not unduly interfere with the rights of others, which would include the rights that any landowner has that flow from ownership.

Public rights of way and statutory access rights are burdens on land of a very unusual kind. Both subsist irrespective of changes in the ownership of the ground, irrespective of the absence of any reference to them in the title deeds or title sheet of the land affected by the rights, and irrespective of whether a new proprietor is aware of their existence. A related observation is that a change in the owner does not automatically change the nature of any access that can be taken under the 2003 Act. It might be that the new owner puts the land to a different use to that which took place before acquisition, which in turn might influence whether land is then excluded from the scope of access rights, but such a development would be at least one step removed from a change in ownership.

Ownership of underlying ground – Additional information

Authority for the statement that ownership of the ground traversed by a public right of way remains unaffected by that is found in the case of *Sutherland* v *Thomson*.[23]

Brief mention can be made of the system of land registration in Scotland, to demonstrate that rights of way and the right of responsible access transcend ownership of the land. This is demonstrated as follows. There is provision to enter details of any public right of way over or through the land into the burdens section of the title sheet of a property, but only insofar as that is known to the Keeper of the Land Register.[24] There is also provision for the particulars of any path order made under section 22 of the 2003 Act to be similarly entered.[25] For our purposes, it is telling that the relevant legislation then goes on to state that the Keeper provides no warranty in relation to whether land is unencumbered by either a right of way or a path order,[26] which means no one can take the absence of these from the Land Register as a guarantee that there are none.

Where next? An introduction to what and where access is allowed

In simple terms, a public right of way can only be used for *passage* along a *given route*. The right of responsible access is comparatively wider. It allows people to be on land for certain purposes and provides a separate right to cross land in a manner that is not restricted to a given route.

The purposes for which someone can enter, stay on, then leave land are for recreation, education and certain commercial activities. As we shall see, such access can be taken to a wide variety of land. (There is a special regime for golf courses such that only the right to cross land applies on areas sculpted for golfing use, and putting greens are specifically excluded even from the right to cross land. All of this will be discussed in detail in the next chapter.)

Public rights of way will not be of much assistance for access takers seeking recreational, educational or commercial access to land. At first glance, it also seems that the right to cross land under the 2003 Act is more flexible than a public right of way, which is restricted to a fixed route. This raises an important question: are public rights of way still important? This can be answered in the affirmative, but rather than simply direct the reader to the relevant chapter of this guide at this stage (which for reference is chapter 3), it is worth briefly considering how, and most importantly where, rights of way can still apply when statutory access rights do not.

One reason has already been alluded to, namely the fact that some land can be excluded from the scope of the right of responsible access. Suppose the main route through a glen is a right of way through a farm steading. As we shall see in more detail in chapter 2, statutory access rights would not apply within the farm steading, much like they would not apply to land where crops are growing. The right of way would therefore be essential to gain access to the glen.

Other situations also serve to highlight the continued importance of public rights of way. Access rights may be restricted for land management reasons, but rights of way cannot be so restricted. That highlights one scenario where a right of way is decidedly less transient than access rights under the 2003 Act. Another was alluded to above, namely where a (new?) landowner decides to do something different with land, such as building a structure on land that was previously open to access. That activity will be regulated by law (most notably planning law), but in most situations the 2003 Act will not regulate that directly. This would mean that the exact spot where access rights could be exercised the year before the erection of a building would no longer be suitable for responsible access during its construction and while it remains standing. Matters could be decidedly different where a public right of way is concerned, as direct legal steps could be taken to preserve the right of way (beyond any general representations in the planning law process). Meanwhile, rights of way can apply to vehicles in some cases, but the general rights of access specifically exclude all motorised access, other than motorised access taken by someone who requires motorised assistance to take access owing to a disability.

Chapter 2 of this guide will now consider the right of responsible access. This overview might have already demonstrated why the right of responsible access is not actually suitable for a particular access activity, in which case you can skip to chapter 3. The right of responsible access does merit prior coverage though, as the wide geographic scope and the wide range of activities caught by the legislation means it is the primary legal regime for many modern access issues.

2
Access Rights Under The 2003 Act

Access rights: an introduction

The possibility of rights of way facilitating access for anyone travelling from point to point along a defined route has been highlighted already. These rights of way and other traditional rights of access will be explored in chapter 3. For now, though, let us imagine a situation where someone wants to take a diversion away from a known public right of way, or simply does not know if a right of way exists but still wishes to take access. Alternatively, someone might wish to do something beyond exercising a right of passage. Can this person be confident such actions will be unchallengeable?

Absent any agreement or tolerance by the landowner, the traditional Scots law position is that a landowner can take steps to retain or regain exclusive possession. Retention of possession might involve the erection of a fence, gate, or any other structure that complies with planning law or other forms of regulation. As for possible steps to regain possession, those will be considered further in chapter 4 (below), but for now it can be noted that a landowner could follow proper (court) procedures to recover vacant possession and regulate any future incursions. For a prohibition of access relative to a specific individual to carry force of law, a court action must be raised against that individual. Furthermore, any civil liability (which might require payment of a sum of money) against a one-time, uninvited visitor will normally be restricted to actual damage caused to the land. When it comes to the criminal law, liability will normally be restricted to actual damage caused, unless a separate offence has been committed. (In special circumstances that offence might be related to the place of access, such as a railway line, or the manner of access, including public order offences.)

Whilst that underlying position remains, the important change brought in by the 2003 Act covers the whole of Scotland, subject to limited exceptions, with rights to access land for passage, recreation, education, and (some) commercial or for-profit activities. These access rights allow people acting responsibly, perhaps accompanied by an animal or using a non-motorised vehicle, to be on land for certain purposes, or to cross land. They are rights for everyone. No prior bargain or even acquiescence by a landowner or manager is required for *ad hoc* use, nor is prior conduct needed to evidence the rights.

The Scottish rights of public access allow people to be above and below land, as well as on the surface of the land itself. Individuals can be there for the duration of a recreational activity, a relevant educational activity relating to the understanding of Scotland's natural or cultural heritage, and even for commercial purposes, provided that the money-making activity can also be undertaken 'otherwise than commercially or for profit'. There is also a stand-alone right to cross land.

This important reform means there will now be many circumstances where a landowner cannot simply regain possession from a responsible access taker on a whim. There are even rules that stop a landowner from blocking off responsible access to land. In this context, the cultural and legal importance of the 2003 Act cannot be overstated. This chapter will consider how these rules work and how both access takers and landowners can stay within the terms of the law. Notable provisions covered will include those which explain what is (and is not) responsible access, the specific areas of land that are excluded from the scope of access rights, and the access-related duties of landowners where access rights can be exercised.

It might be useful to keep in mind that the provisions which set out what land is completely excluded from access rights have a certain primacy. This is because there is no scope for someone to argue that access is responsible when the land itself is excluded from the scope of access rights, as with buildings, suitably-sized domestic gardens, or land on which crops have been sown or are growing. That being said, the structure adopted by the 2003 Act, and accordingly this guide, is to explain the purposes for which access can be taken, after which it makes sense to consider what activities cannot be undertaken, before considering where access cannot be taken at all.

All statutory references in this chapter are to the 2003 Act, unless otherwise stated. Throughout this chapter, the term 'owner' or 'landowner' may refer to either the registered proprietor or a person who has full control over what happens on land (for example, an agricultural tenant). This follows the approach of the 2003 Act itself, which defines 'owner' in this way.

Access rights: comparator countries

For readers with experience of access to land regimes in different countries or with an in interest in learning more about that, a certain analogy can be made between Scottish access rights and the access regimes in Scandinavian countries, including the Swedish *allemansrätten* and the Finnish *jokamiehenoikeus* (which both translate as 'every man's right'), and the Norwegian *friluftsliv* ('open air life'). In these countries, provided the access taker does not fall foul of criminal law (perhaps by causing damage to property or sensitive habitats), these liberal access regimes allow a variety of activities to take place, such as hiking, skiing and camping.

A more limited analogy can be made with the English and Welsh regime under the Countryside and Rights of Way Act 2000, sometimes called the 'CRoW Act', as supplemented by the Marine and Coastal Access Act 2009. The CRoW Act only applies to certain access land (such as mountain, moor, heath or down, where it has been mapped as that). This means that the English and Welsh regime covers a smaller geographic proportion of land than Scottish access rights, even with the later addition of a coastal access network. It also covers a smaller range of (purely recreational) activities.

The Scottish Outdoor Access Code

The Access Code was mentioned in chapter 1. It plays a crucial role in determining what is responsible conduct for access takers and land managers. It also offers explanations or elaborates on the words of the 2003 Act to explain matters, and draws together observations on other relevant areas of law.

When dealing with it, it is important to remember that the Access Code is not law: it declares this itself in paragraph 1.5. Meanwhile, where it is not addressing matters that are related to its core purpose – namely what is responsible conduct – the provisions of the Code must be treated more as guidelines than as actual rules. It does not, for example, lay down an authoritative statement of what land should be treated as excluded from the scope of access rights. It also cannot be treated as authoritative on matters that are not governed by access rights, so its observations on where to park a car carry no particular force in terms of allowing a vehicle to be parked.

Even with that disclaimer, it remains an important document which many sectors of society fed into and which was approved by the Scottish Parliament. Passages of it have been approved in court, and it must be afforded due respect. Further, any observations that do not seem relevant at first might still be relevant to responsible conduct in a less obvious way: for example, directions as to where to leave a car might not be thought of as an authorisation, but rather to clarify that leaving a car in a way that blocks the access of others (either when accessing land yourself or when managing land) will not be responsible.

What activity can the public carry out?

The statutory rights created by the 2003 Act are wider than mere passage. They are (a) the right to be on land for certain specified purposes and (b) the right to cross that land. The purposes specified in the 2003 Act are recreational purposes, educational activity purposes, and commercial or profit-making activities which the person could carry on otherwise than commercially or for profit.

The act of crossing land is simple to understand, through analogies with public rights of way and private rights of access. Nevertheless, section 1(4) of the 2003 Act explains that crossing land means 'going into it, passing over it and leaving it all for the purpose of getting from one place outside the land to another such place'. Meanwhile, being on land for a particular purpose is explained as meaning '(i) going into, passing over and remaining on it for any of those purposes and then leaving it; or (ii) any combination of those'.

Educational activity is the only purpose that is specifically defined in the 2003 Act. An educational activity is one which a person performs for the purposes of furthering that person's understanding of natural or cultural heritage, or enabling or assisting another person in that same endeavour. 'Cultural heritage' and 'natural heritage' are also defined. Cultural heritage relates to the historic, literary and artistic associations of people, places and landscapes and includes structures and other remains of human activity across the ages. Natural heritage includes animal and plant life supported by land and the physical features and beauty of land.

There is no statutory definition of either recreational activity or of commercial or for profit activity. Indications of what these terms mean are however available. For recreation, the Access Code suggests that this includes activities such as walking, cycling, orienteering, climbing and wild camping. It will be recalled from chapter 1 that the Code is an important document that has been approved by the Scottish Parliament. It has a specific role in the context of responsible access to land and it shall be returned to below. There has not been any particular litigation about what constitutes recreational purposes, but one case highlights that camping on land for an extended period of time with a political purpose in mind is not recreational access.[1]

As for 'commercial or for profit' activity, the 2003 Act provides that this must be activity which is capable of being carried out on a non-profit basis. This would include a guide leading tours of mountains, a kayak instructor and arguably a professional landscape photographer (a point discussed in 'additional information' below), because such access takers could undertake this work either commercially or as a hobby. (There might also be ancillary educational purposes to these pursuits.) However, where a commercial activity cannot be carried on for no financial reward it will be excluded. An excluded commercial activity would be sale of goods because this, by definition, requires payment. The setting up of an ice cream stall on Ben Nevis would accordingly be excluded.

As discussed below, some activities are excluded from access rights by the terms of the 2003 Act, even if they might otherwise be classed as (for example) recreation. There may also be criminal law rules that regulate a specific access activity. Activities that cannot be undertaken will be considered shortly.

What activity can the public carry out? – Additional information

Relevant educational activity is defined in section 1(5). It allows both learner and teacher to access the relevant heritage area. Both cultural heritage and natural heritage are defined in section 32, as follows:

> 'cultural heritage' includes structures and other remains resulting from human activity of all periods, traditions, ways of life and the historic, artistic and literary associations of people, places and landscapes.
> 'natural heritage' includes the flora and fauna of land, its geological and physiographical features and its natural beauty and amenity.

The above examples of recreational activities are drawn from paragraph 2.7 of the Access Code, which gives four categories and examples within those categories, namely:

1. pastimes (watching wildlife, sightseeing, painting, photography and enjoying historic sites);
2. family and social activities (short walks, dog walking, picnics, playing, sledging, paddling or flying a kite);
3. active pursuits (walking, cycling, horse riding and carriage driving, rock climbing, hill-walking, running, orienteering, ski touring, ski mountaineering, caving, canoeing, swimming, rowing, windsurfing, sailing, diving, air sports and wild camping); and
4. participation in events (walking or cycling festivals, hill running races, mountain marathons, mountain biking competitions, long-distance riding events).

The 'commercial or for profit' purpose can sometimes be difficult to conceptualise and the statutory introduction seems somewhat circular. The exact wording of the statute is that the right to be on land may be exercised 'for the purposes of carrying on, commercially or for profit, an activity which the person exercising the right could carry on otherwise than commercially or for profit.' Activities that are inherently about making money are therefore excluded. In an article in the Scots Law Times, Cusine suggests that commercial photography or filming can be justified under this provision.[2] This view is consistent with the legislation. In some circles, it has been suggested that photography or filming must be linked to a relevant educational activity. There is no reason to adopt such a restricted interpretation.[3]

Specific criminal offences can operate in relation to any given activity. For example, metal detectorists must have the written consent of Historic Environment Scotland to use a detector in a protected heritage site.[4] It would be impractical to set out all possible examples of offences in this guide. Access takers should consider carefully whether any chosen activity has a specific regulatory regime. Annex 1 of the Access Code is useful here.

What activity can the public *not* carry out?

The access rights conferred by the 2003 Act were not born free. After setting out that everyone has access rights and the purposes for which they can be used, the 2003 Act provides that access rights must be exercised responsibly. The centrality of the concept of responsible access to the operation of the legislative scheme is immediately apparent: sometimes rights of access under the 2003 Act are referred to as the 'right to roam', but a more legally-accurate moniker is the 'right of responsible access'. This is legally and culturally important: anyone asserting a right of responsible access is simultaneously acknowledging that the right is qualified, whereas anyone asserting a right to roam is (erroneously) asserting an unqualified right.

A means of determining what is responsible is therefore important. The mechanism provided in the statute is as follows.

First, it sets out a presumption of responsible access where a person exercises access rights without unduly interfering with the rights of any other person. Those rights do not just mean rights associated with landownership. The access rights of other people are also relevant. This could mean an access taker will need to adjust his plans if another access taker is already taking responsible access to a spot that he also wishes to access. This might mean waiting for that activity to finish, or even reflecting on whether further access to that spot is appropriate for the time being, especially if the terrain or the wildlife in the area is particularly sensitive.

The law then explains that, notwithstanding that presumption, a person cannot be taken as exercising access rights responsibly when acting:

(i)   in contravention of section 9, which contains a banned list of activities which can never be classed as responsible;
(ii) in contravention of any relevant byelaws made under section 12(1)(a)(i); or
(iii) in a manner that undermines any work undertaken by the statutory body SNH (in connection with its role to protect natural and cultural heritage).

Of these, section 9 has the greatest practical effect. It contains seven conduct-based exceptions, such as crossing land in a motorised vehicle where that vehicle is not being used to provide mobility for a person with a disability, and hunting, shooting or fishing. It is analysed in detail below. The second exclusion is context specific, depending on what steps an access authority has taken to regulate the area it is responsible for. The third exclusion relates to the work undertaken by SNH to maintain the natural heritage of land (by putting up and maintaining notices). Such notices must be respected by access takers.

If an access taker's conduct is not caught by these exclusions, whether that conduct is responsible will turn on an analysis of the circumstances. That analysis – which is made on an objective basis – is to have regard to whether an access taker has been following the guidance on responsible conduct in the Access Code and with reference to four aspects relevant to responsibility, specifically highlighted in section 2(3) of the 2003 Act: lawfulness; reasonableness; proper account of the interests of others; and the features of the land in question.

One point to keep in mind is that the access rights are designed for people, not for inanimate objects. (Animals, as shall be seen below, can accompany a human access taker.) Whilst an access taker can bring moveable items with him when accessing land, and a logical case can be made for leaving items briefly and safely unattended during a permitted activity, he must gather these items up when the activity is completed. It is accordingly both sensible, and polite, to ask landowners for permission before leaving unattended items on land for more than an insignificant amount of time.[5]

Access rights do not allow you to leave your car or another motor vehicle on someone else's land without permission. That permission may take the form of an open invitation to park in a designated area, on a first come, first served basis. A landowner may, through appropriate signage, ask that those who park in an area pay a reasonable fee, and anyone parking will be judged to have accepted the wording of a sign and be contractually bound by the displayed terms and conditions. This will be discussed further in chapter 4.

What activity can the public not carry out? – Additional information

Section 2(1) operates as the check on the access rights conferred by section 1: 'A person has access rights only if they are exercised responsibly'.

Section 2(2) then explains how to determine what is responsible, and there is a presumption of responsible access where a person exercises access rights without causing 'unreasonable interference with any of the rights (whether access rights, rights associated with the ownership of land or any others) of any other person'. Presumptions can be rebutted, and therefore analysing any particular set of circumstances to gauge if the presumption applies would not be the end of that matter anyway, but the 2003 Act specifically explains situations where the presumption cannot even operate. This includes the two situations highlighted above (for local byelaws and the work of SNH) and section 9, analysed below.

Responsible access takes heed of all sorts of rights of other parties, be they landowners, tenants, land managers and gillies (and any guests), statutory undertakers (for example, utility providers), other access takers, individuals using a servitude, or fisherfolk. Whilst there has been no direct case law about competition amongst access takers, one reported case highlighted the issues that can arise when a chosen access activity is responsible when undertaken by one person or a small number of people, but at some point a greater amount of access would not be responsible (in this example, owing to the churning effect of horses' hooves that damaged an access route).[6] Amongst other things, this case highlighted the need for access takers to ensure that the overall pattern of land access remains responsible, failing which the landowner will be entitled to take steps to ensure responsible access for all. There is also the possibility of access takers finding themselves in a situation where their chosen access activity is not compatible with other access takers at the same spot, who may be undertaking the same pursuit or engaging in different but equally legitimate activities.[7] This point will be returned to below when mutual responsibilities of access takers and landowners are considered.

Section 2(2)(b) states that in gauging whether access rights are being exercised responsibly, regard *is* (emphasis added) to be had to whether one or both of the Access Code or certain signage erected by SNH has been disregarded. As regards the latter, this would consider whether any request included in or reasonably implied from a notice put up by SNH under section 29 has been disregarded. Note the mandatory wording: any court dealing with a dispute on this point must consider this.

In addition to taking proper account of the interests of others, section 2(3) provides that access should be 'lawful', 'reasonable' and 'take proper account of the features of the land in question.' This is measured objectively.

Whilst the Access Code explains that motorised access is not permitted under the 2003 Act, it nevertheless addresses issues of car parking. It implores that vehicles are not parked in a way that obstructs access[8] and that cars should not be parked in a field where there are animals.[9] It also highlights that permission should be sought and proper plans made for car parking facilities in relation to big events.[10] None of this amounts to a statutory right to leave a car on someone else's land.

Conduct excluded from access rights

Section 9 of the 2003 Act lists seven instances which can never be classed as responsible access. These are:

(a) Being on or crossing land in breach of an interdict or other order of a court;
(b) Being on or crossing land for the purposes of doing anything which is an offence or a breach of an interdict or order of a court;
(c) Hunting, shooting or fishing;

(d) Being on or crossing land while responsible for a dog or other animal which is not under proper control;

(e) Being on or crossing land for the purpose of taking away, for commercial purposes or for profit, anything in or on the land;

(f) Being on or crossing land in or with a motorised vehicle or vessel (other than a vehicle or vessel which has been constructed or adapted for use by a person who has a disability and which is being used by such a person);

(g) Being, for any of the purposes set out in section 1(3) [of the 2003 Act], on land which is a golf course.

Section 9 is largely self-explanatory, but further explanation is helpful for some of its bullet points.

For (a) and (b), an interdict is essentially an order of a Scottish court to refrain from doing something, roughly equivalent to an English injunction.

For (c), the wording of this exclusion will not catch someone who is using the right of responsible access to cross land on the way to a permitted hunting, shooting or fishing activity.

For (e), the clarification that it will never be responsible to take away anything in or on the land commercially should *not* be taken as an open invitation to do this non-commercially in any circumstance. First, it can be noted that items growing on or attached to land will normally be owned by the owner of the land. Second, it is important to remember that the removal of certain plants is a regulated matter (which could, in turn, activate exclusion (b) and the general requirement in section 2(3) of the 2003 Act that responsible access is lawful). The phrasing of this provision was debated in the Scottish Parliament. It is framed so as to not target a casual walker who picks brambles or mushrooms for her own use rather than commercial purposes. A similar rule prevails in Sweden.

For (f), it can safely be inferred that access taken through non-motorised means is not automatically excluded. Access via (for example) a pedal bike or a kayak is subject to the usual requirement of responsible access.

Owing to the importance of the exclusions found in (d) (dogs) and (g) (golf) these are dealt with in standalone segments below. Incidentally, the draftsperson is to be commended for the alphabetical symmetry of relating bullet point (d) to dogs and bullet point (g) to golf.

Conduct excluded from access rights – Additional information

For (b), it should be noted that the offence or breach of court order need not take place on the ground which is being crossed. This means that A could not rely on access rights to be on B's land on his way to burgle C's house.

For (c), a subtle distinction in the wording is apparent, which contrasts with the others by not commencing with the words 'being on or crossing land. . .'. As such, someone crossing A's land in order to fish legally on B's water should not be prohibited from doing so.

For (d), from a statutory interpretation point of view it is curious that dogs are mentioned alongside a general mention of animals, but from a practical perspective this makes some sense owing to the issues with, and indeed prevalence of, dogs. Access rights and dogs are dealt with in the next segment.

For (e), the Scots law process whereby things growing on or attached to land is called accession. The fruit of things that grow on land, such as apples from an apple tree, will in turn be owned by the owner of the land both when they are growing on the tree and after they fall from the tree, through a process called accession by fruit. Picking wild flowers could be an offence under section 13 of the Wildlife and Countryside Act 1981. Reference was made above to Sweden, where the *allemansrätten* (every man's right) prevails.[11] Amidst its liberal access regime, there have been ongoing issues about wild berries.[12] This is highlighted not to offer any solution, but rather to note the issue is not exclusively Scottish.

For (f), it can be noted that driving a motor vehicle off road without lawful authority is an offence under section 34 of the Road Traffic Act 1988, as highlighted in the Access Code, although it can also be noted that it is not an offence for a person to drive a vehicle on his own land, even if he does not have a driving licence. Non-motorised access is catered for in the Code. Horse riding is not specifically mentioned in the statute but in a case involving equine access no issue was raised about whether horse riding was allowed.[13] The Code proceeds on the basis it is, as indeed is a cart drawn by horses (or dogs).[14] An unruly horse could be caught by the exclusion in 9(d). Pedal cycles are not caught by this exclusion. Responsible cycling is covered in the Code;[15] at the other end of the cycling behaviour spectrum, there is also a common law charge of reckless or furious driving of a vehicle or riding of a cycle. It is rarely used, but it is not restricted to roads (as would be the case with the offence of riding a cycle on a road recklessly or without due care and attention under sections 28 and 29 of the Road Traffic Act 1988) and as such could be used where the status of a track as a road is unclear.[16]

Staying with (f), a question mark might be raised about bicycles which are not wholly propelled by human motive power, particularly those that use an electric motor in a way that helps to propel the vehicle forward when a cyclist pedals. A first point to note is that the 2003 Act does not provide for gradations of vehicles, which seems to suggest a vehicle is either motorised or non-motorised. More importantly, it is also noteworthy that the Road Traffic Regulation Act 1984 and the Road Traffic Act 1988 have provision whereby certain vehicles are not to be treated as motor vehicles,[17] but this relaxation applies for the purposes of those statutes and the other Road Traffic Acts only.[18] This means that the rules from the Electrically Assisted Pedal Cycles Regulations 1983,[19] which serve to classify vehicles that would otherwise be motorised as non-motorised, cannot automatically be applied to the 2003 Act (and anyone seeking such an application would have the difficult task of explaining why the 2003 Act was so related to the road traffic regime as to merit a similar interpretation). Whilst it seems unlikely such bicycles were intended to be the target of section 9(f), it is accordingly by no means clear that they are not motorised in terms of the 2003 Act. Future clarification of the statute would be beneficial.

Regarding (g), the exclusion of recreational, educational and commercial activities from the scope of access rights at golf courses is considered below.

Conduct excluded from access rights: dogs not under proper control

There is no statutory right of access to be on land or to cross land where the person wishing to take access is responsible for a dog or other animal which is not under proper control. In determining whether a dog is under proper control, there is no absolute rule that a dog is to be kept on a lead, but in most cases it will be easier to demonstrate that a dog is under control if it is on a lead or, in the case of dogs pulling a vehicle, in harness. The Access Code contains guidance on responsible access with dogs. There has been some discussion around the introduction of legislation to the Scottish Parliament relating to the proper control of dogs (in the context of livestock worrying, which might prescribe usage of leads around live-stock), although no bill has been introduced yet.

Conduct excluded from access rights: dogs not under proper control – Additional information

The Access Code dedicates several paragraphs to access with dogs. It does so because it (rightly) notes that walking a dog can be 'the main opportunity for many people to enjoy the outdoors, to feel secure in doing so and to add to their health and well-being'.[20] Dog walking has implications for others though, and so the Code goes on to explain how to take access with a dog responsibly in general and, in some specific situations, in detail.[21] The general advice is to: (i) not take your dog into a field where there are young animals; (ii) not take your dog into a field of vegetables or fruit (unless you are on a clear path); (iii) keep your dog on a short lead or (where appropriate) under close control; and (iv) remove any faeces left by your dog in a public open place. (Not following the last piece of advice is criminalised under the Dog Fouling etc. (Scotland) Act 2003 (asp 12), and as such there would be responsible access implications for unlawful activity anyway.)

As shall be seen below, despite the Access Code's clear instruction about not taking a dog into a field where there are young animals, there is no general exclusion of fields with livestock from access rights. Dogs in fields with livestock can nevertheless be problematic. Worrying of livestock (which includes a dog simply being at large in a field of sheep) is a crime under the Dogs (Protection of Live-stock) Act 1953. As noted above, this is an area that might be subject to further regulation in the future. While there is no Scottish Government bill planned on the matter, a member's bill is a possibility.

It is perhaps unfortunate that the statute repetitiously uses the word 'responsible' in the context of being 'responsible for' an animal:

in the statutory formulation, it is not responsible access to be responsible for a dog that is not under proper control.

If a dog or other animal causes danger or injury to another person in a public place or gives rise to reasonable cause for alarm or annoyance the person with charge of the animal may commit a criminal offence.[22]

There is no upper limit to the number of dogs that can accompany an access taker, but it is submitted that the ease of determining whether a dog is under proper control will normally be inversely proportionate to how many dogs are with an access taker. Those involved in commercial dog walking activities, who are in the business of exercising other people's dogs, should be especially aware of this. They might also be subject to other regulation depending on how their business is conducted, such as the Animal Boarding Establishments Act 1963.

Conduct excluded from access rights: activities on a golf course other than passage

Section 9(g) is framed negatively, but in effect it confirms that the crossing of land which forms part of a golf course is permitted. What is excluded is being on land which is a golf course for any of the purposes set out in section 1(3) of the 2003 Act (that is to say, recreational, educational or certain commercial purposes). This means that playing a game of frisbee on a fairway or stopping to build a sandcastle in a bunker would not be responsible access. The term 'golf course' is not defined but is readily understood by most people in Scotland. It would include the tees, fairways, rough, bunkers and water traps on a course. It would not automatically include all the land that a golf club or relevant landowning entity dedicated to golf happens to own, so a case could be made for recreational access to woodland at the periphery of a course or educational access to a natural heritage feature that does not form part of the course despite this provision, although this will very much depend on the circumstances. Finally, as we shall see, access to putting greens is completely excluded under a different section of the 2003 Act, meaning that it is not permissible even to cross greens.

**Conduct excluded from access rights: activities on a golf course
other than passage – Additional information**

In the case of *Caledonian Heritable Limited* v *East Lothian Council*
the sheriff considered the point of differing forms of access at a golf
course. When it was suggested to her that different parts of the golf
course might be used for recreational, educational or other activities,
she was sceptical. It is submitted that she was correct to be sceptical,
as there will be many circumstances when to regard a golf course as
anything other than a whole would be problematic.[23] That being the
case, and as acknowledged by the sheriff, this will be context specific
(for example, matters will be different if the course is bisected by a
public highway). It is also submitted that (for example) woodland
at the periphery of the golf course could properly be used for
purposes other than crossing land where that is appropriate in the
circumstances, although this would not be the case for a copse of
trees in the middle of a course, which might be as much of a hazard
as a bunker.

The fact that golf courses (except for greens) are susceptible to
access under the 2003 Act – even though the access is restricted in
scope as compared to non-golf courses – means that those managing
golf courses must do so in a way that respects the right to cross land
in order for that management to be classed as responsible. This is
considered further below.

Where are the rights exercisable?

In addition to the manner of purported access, the place must also
be considered to ensure that access remains under the auspices of
the 2003 Act. Access rights are potentially exercisable on all of Scotland's terrain, except for land that is excluded under section 6. Many
exclusions operate automatically, some operate in certain circumstances only. It is also possible for the relevant access authority to
follow a dedicated procedure to exclude a particular area of land for
a finite but potentially rolling period under section 11.

The starting point is that access rights are exercisable above, below
and on the surface of 'land'. Thus, (non-motorised) airborne and

speleological pursuits are acceptable, including activities such as potholing and paragliding, subject to any regulations governing the use of airspace. Land is defined as including bridges and other structures built on or over land, inland waters, canals and the foreshore which is between the high and low water marks of the ordinary spring tides. This definition comprises most rural areas and could extend to some suburban areas. There is, however, a statutory list of specific types of land over which access rights are not exercisable. Ministers may modify these. The current exclusions are set out below.

Where are the rights exercisable? - Additional information

Section 1(6) states 'Access rights are exercisable above and below (as well as on) the surface of the land.' Where water is concerned, this means they can be exercised on the surface as well as underwater. Section 1(7) provides 'the land in respect of which access rights are exercisable is all land except that specified in or under section 6 . . .'. The definition of land is in section 32. By including 'bridges and other structures built on land' it appears, at first glance, wide enough to include buildings. (This would also align with the Scots property law process called accession whereby things attach to, and become part of, land.) As shall be seen below, the statute introduces an exception for structures to prevent this happening.

Land excluded from access rights

Section 6 is the important provision that dictates the geography of access rights across Scotland. Where it operates, even an impeccably behaved access taker cannot rely on the 2003 Act.

Within section 6 and the supplementary section 7 (which clarifies aspects of section 6) there are different types of exclusion. The exclusion may operate automatically, owing to the characteristics of the land, or it may operate from time to time, when land is being used for a purpose it has been landscaped for.

Subsection (1) of section 6 lists exclusions in ten paragraphs (a)–

(j). These provisions, listed in the next segment, can be rendered for ease as fifteen situations where access rights are excluded. Amongst those exclusions is the local authority power to exempt land from access (under section 11), which is analysed in detail below. For now, it can be noted that access authorities are encouraged to use this power sparingly, in line with the Guidance for Local Authorities and National Park Authorities published by the Scottish Executive (the former name for the Scottish Government) in 2005 (available at www.gov.scot/Publications/2005/ 02/20645/51835).

Section 6 exclusions to access rights do not apply to land that is a core path, save in very particular circumstances. These are when access must be restricted owing to an outbreak of animal disease and where access has been suspended by an access authority under section 11.

Under section 8 of the 2003 Act, Scottish Ministers have power to modify the provisions relating to access exclusions. This power has already been used to clarify provisions about growing crops (to provide that access to areas where trees are being cultivated in beds is excluded but other wooded areas are not) and to allow for the suspension of access rights in relation to core paths in certain circumstances.

Brief mention should also be made of powers to restrict access for defence or national security. Although deployment of these rules will not be a day-to-day occurrence, the Secretary of State for Scotland has the ability to exclude land if he is satisfied that it is necessary so to do for the purposes of defence or national security (under the Land Reform (Scotland) Act 2003 (Directions for the Purposes of Defence or National Security) Order 2003 (SI 2003/2250)).

Where land is not specifically excluded by the 2003 Act, it is not for a landowner or land manager to unilaterally decide such land should in fact be excluded from access rights, even if the landowner owns further land nearby and has not restricted access to that further land. There might be land management reasons to restrict access in some circumstances, which are considered below, but the status of land as access land is set by law rather than the landowner.

Land excluded from access rights – Additional information

As noted, sections 6 and 7 operate to determine exactly where access rights can be exercised. This has led some people (including the author)[24] to describe disputes about the scope of these rules as 'where' cases and disputes about whether a particular access activity is (or was) responsible as 'how' cases. Whilst this can be a useful device, it is not a wholly accurate categorisation exercise, as some of the 'where' exceptions (for example, relating to land dedicated to sport) only apply from time to time, and moreover if a limitation on how land may be used for access is upheld that could have the practical effect of barring many or all forms of access taking on land.[25] That critique aside, it might assist with understanding how the regime works, and the focus of this additional information is firmly on the 'where' rather than the 'how'. Where a 'where' exclusion applies, there is no scope to even argue about the 'how'.

Section 6 generally does not apply to land designated as a core path, which means an access taker and a landowner can normally be sure access rights exist over core paths. The circumstances in which section 6 can apply to core paths are where public access is prohibited or restricted by or under any enactment in consequence of an outbreak of animal disease (such as 'foot and mouth' disease) and where a local authority has specified that access over the core path is to be suspended under section 11 (which can only be done if there has been due consideration of the core path).[26] In January 2014, the Scottish Government revised the guidance that was published in 2005 to take into account a change in the law to accommodate the temporary closure of core paths.[27]

To the extent that there was any uncertainty about whether a landowner or land manager could render a parcel of land as excluded from access by simply enclosing it where no specific exclusion applied to that area, this has been clarified by the recent Court of Session case of *Renyana Stahl Anstalt* v *Loch Lomond and the Trossachs National Park Authority*[28]. In that case, notwithstanding the fact that an enclosure was part of a larger area (and access was possible in that larger area), the enclosed land in question was clearly not excluded as a single unit and so could not be carved out for separate treatment. Within the enclosed area there were some features (such as farm buildings) that could have been exempt from access (paragraph 55), and indeed future features could also have led to the exemption of areas of ground, but any restriction relating to the whole enclosed area would need to be part of a properly considered – and objectively justifiable (see below) – overall land management scheme.[29]

Land excluded from access rights: specific exclusions

The fifteen situations where access rights are excluded by the operation of section 6 are as follows.

(i) *Land on which there is erected a building or other structure or works, plant or fixed machinery.* In this context, the law provides that 'a bridge, tunnel, causeway, launching site, groyne, weir, boulder weir, embankment of a canalised waterway, fence, wall or anything designed to facilitate passage is not to be regarded as a structure', meaning that access can be taken over or through those features.

(ii) *Land on which there is a caravan, tent or other place affording a person privacy or shelter.*

(iii) *Land which forms the curtilage of a building which is not a house (or the curtilage of a group of buildings, none of which is a house).*

(iv) *Land which forms a compound or other enclosure containing any such structure, works, plant or fixed machinery as is referred to in (i) above.*

(v) *Land which is contiguous to and used for the purposes of a school.*

(vi) *Land which comprises in relation to a house or any of the places mentioned in (ii) above sufficient adjacent land to enable persons living there to have a reasonable measure of privacy in that house or place and to ensure that their enjoyment is not unreasonably disturbed.* This means suitably sized domestic gardens are excluded, as explained below.

(vii) *Land which is owned in common and used by two or more persons as a private garden.* As such, the ornamental squares in Edinburgh are excluded where they are owned in common, as further explained below.

(viii) *Land to which public access is prohibited, excluded or restricted under an enactment.* This means public rights of access do not permit e.g. the public to walk along railway lines.

(ix) *Land which has been developed or set out as a sports or playing field or for a particular recreational purpose, either while in use as such or in some circumstances on a permanent basis.* Note the special treatment of golf courses, which was considered above, and also note that this exclusion does not apply in relation to many arrangements designed to facilitate fishing, discussed below.

(x) *Land to which for not fewer than 90 days in the year ending on 31st January 2001 members of the public were permitted only on payment* and *(emphasis added) after that date for not fewer than 90 days in each year beginning on 1st February 2001 members of the public are, or are to be, so admitted.*

(xi) *Land on which building, civil engineering or demolition works or other works are being carried out.*

(xii) *Land on which works are being carried out by a statutory undertaker for the purposes of the undertaking.*

(xiii) *Land which is used for the working of minerals by surface workings including quarrying.*

(xiv) *Land on which crops have been sown or are growing.* Note that this provision has a specific meaning when it comes to grassland and orchards and does not include headrigs, endrigs and other margins of fields, discussed below.

(xv) *Land which has been specified in an order under section 11 of the 2003 Act or byelaws under section 12 as land in respect of which access rights are not exercisable.*

Section 6 is not the whole story. Section 7 provides further clarification, noting (for example) what is meant by a 'school', what the role of planning law is when determining whether a feature on land can be treated as an excluded area, whether land dedicated to sport is excluded on a temporary or permanent basis, and also what the relevant considerations are when determining how big a garden is appropriate in terms of situation (vi). It also makes clear that section 6 exclusions do not apply to land that is a core path, save in very particular circumstances.

A recurring point of contention in court has been the extent to which domestic ground around a private residence is excluded, under section 6(1)(b)(iv). (That is the sixth scenario listed above, although after this paragraph this guide will revert to the statutory references.) Given its importance and the contention that has surrounded it, it will be analysed in detail below. The effect and related procedure of section 6(1)(j) and section 11 (access authority suspensions) and section 12 (byelaws) also merit standalone analysis away from the automatic section 6 exclusions. Of those, some of the exclusions are comparatively clear: so nothing more needs to be said of section 6(1)(b)(ii) (an enclosure or compound containing works etc., which is item (iv) on the list above), section 6(1)(d) (access regulated by another enactment, listed at (viii) above), section 6(1)(g) (building, civil engineering or demolition works *and* where a statutory under-taker is engaged with its mandated activity, listed at (xi) and (xii) above), and section 6(1)(h) (mineral works on the surface, including quarrying, listed at (xiii) above).

Land excluded from access rights: specific exclusions – Additional information

Given the lack of authoritative case law on exclusions other than domestic gardens, an analysis of the remaining exclusions necessarily involves some speculation. Suitable sources will be offered to justify any propositions made. One such source is the Access Code. In this context, the Code should not be treated as definitive, particularly as it has limited standing when it comes to determining what is excluded land.[30] That said, it remains an important document in the overall scheme of the 2003 Act and it has been approved by the Scottish Parliament, and so it does have a unique role.

Section 7 works alongside section 6, so comment on it will be laced through the comments on the corresponding provision in section 6. Brief comment shall also be offered here on section 7(2) and section 7(3), the latter of which contributed to a Court of Session case on an important point of law.

Section 7(2) states that it is not possible to claim that land is within section 6 if to do so would require a development or change of use for which planning permission is needed where such planning permission has not been granted (or it was granted subject to an as yet unfulfilled condition). Section 7(3) then notes that when planning permission has been granted and the corresponding development or change of use is taking place, then for the purposes of section 6 it will be treated as having been developed or having had its use changed. In the lead up to the case of *The Council of the Law Society of Scotland* v *The Scottish Legal Complaints Commission*,[31] a solicitor sent a letter to a couple who had allegedly taken access to his client's land that had (apparently) been the subject of planning permission, pointing out the effect of section 7(3) in forthright terms, albeit without clarifying what steps other than obtaining the planning permission had occurred to demonstrate the development was 'taking place', that being required before any exclusion could apply. In addition to challenging the version of events presented by the solicitor (this aspect of the discussion did not lead to a reported case), the couple complained to the Scottish Legal Complaints Commission about what they called an overly aggressive, intimidating and threatening letter. Eventually that complaint came to nothing,[32] but it was a finely balanced case which now serves as a reminder that solicitors involved in access disputes ought to consider carefully what their role is when corresponding with non-solicitors. It also provides an example of where section 7(3) might come into play.

Land excluded from access rights: specific exclusions; buildings

Under section 6(1)(a) a 'building' is excluded outright. 'Building' is not defined but this will usually be obvious, by dint of having walls (or a circular wall) and a roof.

Land excluded from access rights: specific exclusions; buildings – Additional information

One thing left unsaid in the statute is at what stage an old building stops being a building in the technical sense of the statute and becomes part of cultural heritage. Access is envisaged at such spots, as is clear from the definition of 'cultural heritage',[33] which can be accessed for a relevant educational activity, and in terms of the Access Code.[34] It is impossible to give definitive guidance as to when a building stops being a building and moves into the realms of being cultural heritage.[35] Also covered by this provision are more temporary sheltered places. Caravans and tents are the only shelters specifically mentioned, leaving the status of unsteady bivouacs open to debate.

Land excluded from access rights: specific exclusions – the curtilage of buildings

In addition to buildings being excluded, land that specifically pertains to them is also excluded under section 6(1)(b)(i). The statute uses the word 'curtilage'. This is not defined.

Land excluded from access rights: specific exclusions; the curtilage of buildings – Additional information

The exclusion of the curtilage of a building depends on the existence of a building that is not a house (or a group of buildings none of which is a house). The curtilage of such a building or a group of buildings is excluded. The land around houses is dealt with by the (wider) exclusion in section 6(1)(b)(iv).

As to what 'curtilage' means in the absence of a statutory definition, the Access Code offers the following explanation of the concept:

> It will usually be possible to judge what is the curtilage of a building by the presence of some physical feature such as a wall, fence, an area of hardstanding or some other physical boundary. Where there is no physical feature, you will need to make a judgement about what land is used together with a building.[36]

Further guidance as to what the word signifies might be drawn from attempts to glean its meaning from its appearance in other legislation and interpretations of that,[37] although even with such guidance it is clear that the meaning of the term is highly contextual.

Land excluded from access rights: specific exclusions; schools

Land contiguous to and used for the purposes of a school is excluded. 'School' is given a specific definition. The use of the word 'contiguous' means the land must be part of the same complex as the school (with no need to cross other land) for the exclusion to apply.

Land excluded from access rights: specific exclusions; schools – Additional information

> 'School' is defined as meaning 'not only a school within the meaning of section 135(1) of the Education (Scotland) Act 1980 but also any other institution which provides education for children below school age within the meaning of that provision'.[38] The effect of this additional wording is to bring institutions providing education to children below the age of five into the scope of the exclusion. No other school-like institution is caught. It can also be noted that, for example, playing fields used by a school which are not contiguous to that school will not be caught by this exclusion, but they may be caught by another (such as section 6(1)(e)).

Land excluded from access rights: specific exclusions; gardens owned in common

The exclusion for land which is owned in common and used by two or more persons as a private garden applies where the section 6(1)(b)(iv) does not, meaning that there is no need for land to be adjacent to the place it serves. As such, it will apply to exclude access takers from a shared garden that is not necessarily contiguous to the places it serves.

Land excluded from access rights: specific exclusions; gardens owned in common – Additional information

As noted above, and as envisaged by the Access Code, this exclusion will typically apply to common gardens available to the inhabitants of a street or square in an urban environment.[39] The provision has been subjected to academic critique.[40] From a drafting perspective, it is noticeable that the exclusion for domestic gardens under section 6(1)(b)(iv) does not use the word 'garden', but section 6(1)(c) does.

Land excluded from access rights: specific exclusions; sports or playing fields etc.

What seems like an absolute exclusion of sports or playing fields or ground set out for a particular recreational purpose is decidedly less absolute when considered (as it must be) alongside section 7(7). That explains that the exclusion is only absolute in the case of synthetic sports or playing fields and in relation to particularly sensitive grass areas, namely the four given examples of golf (putting) greens, bowling greens, crickets squares and lawn tennis courts, or the residuary category of a 'similar area on which grass is grown and prepared for a particular recreational purpose'. As four important grass recreational sites have already been identified, there will not be many further recreational activities to be caught, but it is suggested a standard-sized croquet lawn might be. Otherwise, the exclusion only applies when the land is being used for the purpose it has been dedicated for. This means access rights could not be used to cross a grass football pitch or for a game of rounders when it is being used for a football match. For completeness, it should also be recalled that, on a golf course, access rights can only be used to cross the land (under section 9(g)).

This exclusion must also be read alongside section 7(8), relating to arrangements that facilitate fishing. This allows access to land on which groynes have been constructed or platforms erected, where pools have been deepened, or where other works for the purposes of fishing have taken place.

Land excluded from access rights: specific exclusions;
historic and ongoing charging

Section 6(1)(f) allows for historic charging to continue notwithstand-ing the 2003 Act. This would allow, for example, a safari park to continue its commercial operations and charge for access to it.

The statute uses the conjunctive 'and' rather than a disjunctive 'or' – both historic and continuing charges are needed. Note also that charging must have happened 'each year'. This means that a landowner must have been charging for not fewer than 90 days in the year ending on 31st January 2001, i.e. historic fees in a benchmark year, and a charging regime must have continued for not fewer than 90 days in each following year. Any landowner seeking to rely on this grandfathered exclusion will need to be able to suitably evidence it. The date relates to when the first draft Land Reform (Scotland) Bill was published.

Land excluded from access rights: specific exclusions; historic and
ongoing charging – Additional information

It is notable that section 6(1)(f) specifies that it only applies when the charging regime operated (and continues to operate) in a way that admission was (and is) only on payment. This would seem to exclude an admission system based on an 'honesty box' to deposit a suggested contribution. Meanwhile, section 7(9) clarifies that those within a class of persons who have not been required to pay to gain admittance on the relevant days will continue to have access rights; in other words, they will be able to access the land free of charge.

Land excluded from access rights: specific exclusions; crops

There is an exclusion for land where crops have been sown or are growing, but not to fields where there are livestock. In terms of section 7(10), 'crops' means plants which are cultivated for agricultural or commercial purposes. Ground in which crops are growing does not include woodland, orchards or land used mainly for growing trees but does include tree nurseries and land on which tree seeds are sown. Grass only counts as a growing crop when it is being grown for hay or silage and is at such a late stage of growth that it might be damaged by the exercise of access rights. Headrigs, endrigs and other margins of fields in which crops are growing are not excluded from access rights.

Land excluded from access rights: specific exclusions; crops –
Additional information

> The initial version of the statute was quickly amended to cater for concerns relating to forestry.[41] As amended, access takers can normally be confident when accessing mature woodland, subject to any responsible land management that a landowner may be undertaking.

Land excluded from access rights: gardens

Section 6(1)(b)(iv) is an important provision. It seeks to balance someone's right to a private and family life in terms of human rights law with the liberal access regime. It provides that a dwelling should have 'sufficient adjacent land to enable persons living there to have reasonable measures of privacy' and 'to ensure that their enjoyment of that [dwelling] is not unreasonably disturbed.'

The relevant factors include (but are not limited to) the location of and the other characteristics of the dwelling. The exclusion is not restricted to an occupied building. It also extends to a tent, caravan or other place affording a person privacy or shelter, although presumably such a dwelling can expect less of a 'garden' than a building designed as a home with a dedicated outdoor area pertaining to it.

The Access Code uses the term 'garden' for land adjacent to a dwelling, even though this term is not used in the 2003 Act for this purpose. The word is nevertheless useful in bringing to mind what the statute means. The Code also suggests what sort of land the exclusion applies to, highlighting relevant features for determining whether land close to dwelling is a garden:

- a clear boundary (whether man-made or natural);
- manicured grass;
- flowerbeds and tended shrubs;
- paving and water features;
- sheds, glasshouses and summer houses; and
- vegetable and fruit gardens.

Other relevant features that might be volunteered would include wooden decking (by analogy with paving) and washing lines on a drying area that serves a dwelling.

Practical as the suggestions in the Access Code are, they are not definitive. As has been noted above, despite its importance the Code is designed to deal with responsible access to and management of land and as such has limited status when it comes to determining where access rights can be exercised. That is a matter for the courts, and there have been several cases.

Land excluded from access rights: gardens – Additional information

The relevant wording of section 6(1)(b)(iv) which sets up the sufficient adjacent land exclusion is extracted above. Section 7(5) then provides 'There are included among the factors which go to determine what extent of land is sufficient for the purposes mentioned in section 6(1)(b)(iv) . . ., the location and other characteristics of the house or other place.'

The provision itself was drafted with Article 8 of the European Convention on Human Rights in mind, which sets out the human right to private and family life. The drafting has not proved to be problematic in any reported cases; or, to put it another way, the scheme of the 2003 Act already caters for human rights concerns. Reference can also be made to Article 1 of the First Protocol to that Convention, as it guarantees peaceful enjoyment of possessions, but that can be subject to certain controls by a signatory state.

The Scottish regime is inherently flexible and adaptable to a specific setting. This can be contrasted with the English and Welsh access to land regime under the Countryside and Rights of Way Act 2000, which fixes a distance around dwellings situated in access land, giving a 20-metre exclusion zone where access cannot be taken.[42]

As for the role of the Access Code in this exercise, the scepticism with which it has been treated in litigation about this exclusion has already been highlighted. In one case, it was noted that 'it might be going too far to hold that the Code is entirely irrelevant', but also (and more importantly) 'it cannot be said that the advice and guidance given by the Code is a direct help to the interpretation of section 6'.[43] To this, it can be added that the Code's contention that the 'wider, less intensively managed parts of the policies, such as grassland and woodlands, whether enclosed or not, would not be classed as a garden and so access rights can be exercised'[44] has not withstood scrutiny. As Gretton and Steven observe, the 2003 Act 'does not make the *use* of the land the test'.[45] If it did, owners of a big house might be tempted to intensively manage a large area (perhaps by making it a lawn).

Land excluded from access rights: gardens; case law

Every situation is different, but some principles can be drawn from these cases that have taken place.

First, it is the enjoyment of the dwelling itself that is protected, not the enjoyment of any other land. It is also clear that the home-owner/occupier must be measured objectively rather than subjectively. This means that the profile of a person who happens to be the occupier of the dwelling is not relevant. That said, a court might draw inferences about the type of occupier who could be expected to reside in a house from its characteristics.

A previous version of ScotWays guidance noted 'Presumably a larger house may require a larger "garden".' Case law has largely demonstrated this to be correct, although it is not just about how big a house is. The overarching concern brings matters back to what the 2003 Act highlights, namely sufficient adjacent land to allow the occupier(s) reasonable measures of privacy to do all the things anyone can normally expect to do in and around a home. A large house, with large windows, large approaches and expansive 'policies' will occasion legitimate privacy concerns that will unavoidably cover a larger area than a semi-detached house abutting a main road in a suburban environment. Access takers should be sensitive to whichever situation they find themselves in.

The relevant cases are *Gloag* v *Perth and Kinross Council*[46] (hereafter referred to as '*Gloag*') and *Snowie* v *Stirling Council*[47] (hereafter referred to as '*Snowie*'), both of which led to sheriff court rulings that areas slightly in excess of 10 acres around expansive residences near Perth and Stirling respectively were not land in respect of which access rights could be exercised. (In the *Snowie* case a much bigger area was unsuccessfully argued for by the owners.) In the case of *Creelman* v *Argyll and Bute Council*[48] (hereafter referred to as '*Creelman*') a similar but smaller exclusion was found to be appropriate, amounting to six acres of land. Those cases related to rural areas. A non-rural judicial interpretation of this exception was *Forbes* v *Fife Council*[49] (hereafter referred to as '*Forbes*'), which turned on the status of a path on the opposite side of a fence from a house in suburban Glenrothes. This path was found not to be part of the sufficiently adjacent land needed for the privacy of that dwelling, and therefore was not excluded.

Land excluded from access rights: gardens; case law –
Additional information

In *Gloag* the proprietor erected a new fence (following the line of a previous fence) around the grounds to enhance the security of her property. She then applied to the sheriff court under section 28 for a declaration that the land within the fence was not land where access rights were exercisable. The sheriff found in fact that this amounted to about 11 acres of land, although the access authority's maps indicated an overall area of 14.6 acres within the fence. The access authority proposed a smaller area was appropriate, which would have made about 4 acres of woodlands and rough grass available for access. The Ramblers Association, who intervened in the case, took the same approach.

The sheriff adopted an objective test, not related to the particular owner of land at any given time, and so discounted points raised by the landowner about her own specific profile,[50] but proceeded on the basis that an appropriate area should be determined with reference to the reasonable needs and expectations of any person who purchased such a house. The sheriff held that all the land within the fence was excluded from the exercise of access rights. The evidence had shown that the fence had been placed in the most suitable location. The fact that it followed the line of a previous fence showed that it had not been placed along a purely arbitrary line, but one which a previous occupant had considered was required to secure their privacy and enjoyment of the property.

In *Snowie* the landowners (and their tenants)[51] had been served with a notice by the access authority to reopen a gate that had been locked in a way that blocked access that the public had previously enjoyed. In the course of objecting to this, the landowners sought clarification of the extent of land that was excluded from access. They claimed that a substantial part of the 70-acre estate should be excluded, including the entire length of the driveway that had been closed. The sheriff rejected this approach and outlined a smaller area of 12.6 acres that pertained to a house to be excluded, including the rear garden of the house, some tennis courts and changing rooms, and adjacent gardens. Some tenanted houses were also on the estate, which had well-defined garden areas that were excluded from access. As in the *Gloag,* case, an objective approach to the privacy of occupiers was adopted. The decision was initially appealed but the appeal was dropped.

Creelman involved a smaller area, where the landowner owned six acres at Glendaruel, Argyll, on which two buildings were sited. Only four of the six acres were useable as a garden (being the ground between the two buildings). In what the sheriff acknowledged was not a particularly easy case, he held that the whole area was excluded. Again, an objective approach was adopted, and in this analysis the sheriff noted that granting access to any part of the land (which included a path) would have affected the enjoyment of the dwellings there. The factors considered included the relatively small area of the ground (when compared to other properties in the locality), the proximity of the track to the houses, the rural nature of the area and the likelihood that any occupier would value the garden area.[52]

In *Forbes*, an exclusion was sought in relation to a path on the far side of the fence from a row of houses in 'a quiet suburban part of Glenrothes'.[53] The sheriff held the land on the other side of the fence was *not* excluded from access rights. In raw distance terms, this path was closer than much of the land that had been excluded in, for example, *Gloag*, but the occupiers of the house had sufficient privacy owing to the six foot fence and the garden between the house and the fence, which was is 'in reasonably generous proportions but not excessively so'.[54]

The net effect of the cases and the non-occupier specific approach of gauging whether a garden next to a dwelling is excluded has led one commentator to call the assessment exercise the 'property-specific objective test'.[55] This neatly encapsulates the fact that the test is ostensibly objective, but something akin to subjectivity can creep into a consideration of who might live in a specific property.

All of this means that the Scottish regime is inherently flexible and adaptable to a specific setting. This can be contrasted with the English and Welsh position mentioned above.[56]

It is difficult to be specific about when a garden is excluded in the adaptable Scottish regime. Topography is clearly relevant, but only especially useful in cases where clear features exist, such as a dwelling on a small island or bounded by a natural feature like a cliff or watercourse. (The Boquhan Burn and the River Ruel were relevant in *Snowie* and *Creelman* respectively.) The *Gloag* case suggests boundary features designed with the occupier of a dwelling in mind can be relevant and, to an extent, it may even be possible for a landowner to influence topography with some creative landscaping, provided such features or landscaping are not created in a way that falls foul of section 14(1) as an obstruction to access (discussed below). Topography, boundary features and other factors might contribute to a landowner's legitimate security concerns (objectively measured), and such concerns could also be properly considered.

Land excluded from access rights: local authority suspensions

An access authority may, for a specified time, exempt a parcel of land from the access rights which would otherwise be exercisable there, to allow that land to be used for a particular specified purpose. It can do this of its own volition or on application by an interested party. If the suspension is to have effect for six or more days, it must consult and give public notice of the plan. Further, the Scottish Ministers then need to confirm any order, which might involve holding a public inquiry. Public notice of an order must be given by the access authority as soon as practicable after it is made or, where the order requires to be confirmed by Ministers, the authority receive notice of confirmation. An order can have effect for up to two years, but may be renewed. If the order relates to land where there is a core path, it should specify the core path in the order. Such an order has no effect in relation to public rights of way that fall within the designated area. This means a core path which is also public right of way will continue to be accessible for passage along its route.

In 2005, the Scottish Executive (as the Scottish Government was then known) published Guidance for Local Authorities and National Park Authorities (available at www.gov.scot/Publications/2005/02 20645/51835). This includes guidance to access authorities on their power to exempt particular land. The guidance indicates that the reasons for exempting land should be limited to:

• allowing a charge to be levied for admission to a particular event;
• in the interests of safety and security;
• ensuring the protection of privacy, where the other provisions of the Act are deemed to be insufficient to protect privacy.

Events for which appropriate temporary suspensions might be made include a Highland games event, a music festival, a golf tournament, a motor rally, or a high-profile wedding at a country location.

Land excluded from access rights: local authority suspensions – Additional information

Section 11 (and section 6(1)(j)) of the 2003 Act allows for the suspension of all access rights in order facilitate a designated purpose mentioned in an order for a period of up to five days (which will not involve a consultation exercise and confirmation by the Scottish Ministers) or a period from six days up to two years in duration (which will involve consultation and confirmation).[57] The consultation must involve the owner of the land to which it would relate, the relevant local access forum and such other persons as the access authority thinks appropriate. The access authority must also give public notice of the intended purpose and effect of the proposed order, inviting objections to be sent to them within a reasonable time. Objections and any other representations received by the access authority must be considered and passed to the Scottish Ministers. Ministers must also consider these and may cause an inquiry to be held under section 265 of the Town and Country Planning (Scotland) Act 1997. Ministers can confirm the order, with or without modifications, or refuse to confirm it.

The exemption may be restricted to particular times of day, but the exemption is a complete one as regards the suspension of access rights. This means there is no power, for example, to exclude cycling whilst permitting pedestrian access to continue.

Whilst this might seem like an attractive way to suspend access rights, it will not be always be a suitable power to use where there is an ongoing particular need for privacy. This is because the requirement to consult for any application for more than five days on that ground would draw attention to the particular purpose specified in the order.

Land on which access rights are excluded or further regulated: byelaws

In addition to the power to suspend access rights under section 11, access authorities can further regulate or exclude access to land under section 12. Different rules may apply in different locations.

In contrast to the power to suspend access rights, which are intended to be short term and carry with them no criminal sanction, byelaws are not drafted with a time limit in mind and carry criminal sanctions. This means that the Access Code slogan of 'Know the Code before you go' only goes so far when you are going to an area affected by byelaws. You must be aware of local byelaws too.

Byelaws cannot be made in secret. When they are first proposed they must be open to public inspection and consultation with relevant parties must take place. Reference should be made to the guidance to access authorities issued under section 27.

Byelaws can: (a) prohibit, restrict or regulate the exercise of access rights; (b) facilitate their exercise; or (c) prohibit or regulate (i) the use of vehicles or vessels; (ii) the taking place of sporting and recreational activities; (iii) the conduct of any trade or business; (iv) the depositing or leaving of rubbish or litter; and (v) the lighting of fires and the doing of anything likely to cause a fire, on the land. (Steps can be taken under (c) so as to protect and further the interests of access takers and potential access takers.) Any byelaws made under section 12 do not interfere with the exercise of any public right of way or navigation or the functions of a statutory undertaker. This means that a right of passage along a right of way will continue notwithstanding any action under this section: therefore any attempt to bring that right of way to an end would need to follow a different procedure (discussed in chapter 3).

Some byelaws exist in relation to camping at strategic locations in Scotland, such as Holyrood Park in Edinburgh and, most notably, in certain areas of the Loch Lomond and The Trossachs National Park. Those prominent byelaws were actually passed under Paragraph 8 of Schedule 2 to the National Parks (Scotland) Act 2000 (asp 10) (which allows byelaws to be made to regulate the exercise of recreational activities, amongst other things).

Land on which access rights are excluded or further regulated: byelaws – Additional information

For land to be totally excluded from access rights under a byelaw, a parcel of land should be specified as land in respect of which access rights are not exercisable (via section 6(1)(j)).[58] Where land has not been so excluded, certain activities might nevertheless be regulated there, as is the case with the example of the Loch Lomond and The Trossachs National Park Camping Management Byelaws 2017.[59]

An access authority can also use section 12 to make additional provision on the responsible exercise of access rights and the responsible use, management and conduct of the ownership of the land, beyond that which is already stipulated earlier in the 2003 Act.[60]

Interestingly, byelaws can also provide for (i) the preservation of public order and safety; (ii) the prevention of damage; (iii) the prevention of nuisance or danger; (iv) the conservation or enhancement of natural or cultural heritage.[61] Some of these might properly be classed as of national rather than of local concern.

When making byelaws, sections 202 to 204 of the Local Government (Scotland) Act 1973 apply to the procedure (with slight modifications). Consultation must take place with any local community council, the landowner(s), representatives of local people and businesses, the local access forum(s), any relevant statutory undertaker, SNH and anyone else the access authority thinks fit.[62]

Remedies when someone is on excluded land or not responsible

In terms of section 5(1), 'the exercise of access rights does not of itself constitute trespass'. This means a landowner will be unsuccessful in any claim against a responsible access taker on non-excluded land. When someone strays onto excluded land or acts in a way that is not responsible, section 5(1) no longer applies and the landowner can take the usual steps to recover possession unless the person taking access is otherwise entitled to be there (for example, if it is a public right of way). The steps a landowner can take will be considered further in chapter 4. No other penalty is stipulated in the 2003 Act.

Duties of the landowner in relation to accessible land

Every owner of land in respect of which access rights are exercisable has a duty to use and manage the land and otherwise to conduct the ownership of it in a way which, as respects those rights, is responsible, under section 3 of the 2003 Act. It will be recalled 'owner' in this context means the registered landowner and anyone who has a large degree of control over what happens on the land (such as an agricultural tenant), in accordance with section 32 of the 2003 Act.

In this guide, 'land management' will be used as the composite term for 'using, managing and conducting the ownership of land'.

What is 'responsible'? This is assessed in a similar way to responsible access. An owner is presumed to be managing land in a way which is responsible if it does not cause unreasonable interference with the access rights of any person exercising or seeking to exercise them. There are then certain things that can never be responsible land management, namely contravention of section 14(1) or (3) (access impediments, and the related provision where an access authority issues a notice to remove impediments), section 23(2) (reinstatement of a core path or a right of way after ploughing or other disturbance) or any byelaw made under section 12. These are considered below.

If an owner is not caught by these exclusions, whether that conduct is responsible will turn on an analysis of the circumstances.

That analysis is to have regard to whether any act or omission by the owner 'disregards the guidance on responsible conduct set out in the Access Code and incumbent on the owners of land' and with reference to the three aspects relevant to responsibility specifically highlighted in section 3(3) of the 2003 Act: lawfulness; reasonableness; and taking proper account of the interests of others.

There have been several cases which offer guidance on what a landowner can do to manage land. All have involved an access authority reacting to a perceived contravention of section 14(1) by a landowner. These will be considered in more detail below. For now, it can be noted that one case – *Tuley* v *The Highland Council*[63] – provides authority that it can be responsible land management to zone land for certain activities, such as by steering equestrian access to a particular route whilst excluding horse riders from a path that is susceptible to damage by ongoing equestrian access. Another case – *Renyana Stahl Anstalt* v *Loch Lomond and the Trossachs National Park Authority*[64] – highlights the importance of the Access Code in measuring what is responsible land management and confirms that it is mandatory to have regard to it when assessing, on an objective basis, what is responsible.

Land managers should pay heed to Part 4 of the Access Code, entitled 'Managing Land and Water Responsibly for Access'. Practical suggestions as to how a landowner can respect access rights when managing land or water include (but are not limited to): (i) not purposefully or unreasonably stopping or discouraging the exercise of access rights on or off paths and tracks; (ii) using paths and tracks as a way of managing access across land so that access is integrated with land management (and working with the access authority and other bodies); and (iii) keeping the public informed about (and making suitable alternative access arrangements for) land management operations whilst keeping anything that might impinge on access to a minimum area and duration. Where notices are necessary, these should be in obvious places, and simple 'no access' signs should be avoided. The locking or removal of gates or other access points should also be avoided, particularly on paths or tracks likely to be used by the public, although the provision of a reasonable alternative means of access may offset that.

Where a landowner is not actually in contravention of the strict terms of section 14, section 23 or any byelaws, a question arises as to what remedies exist for disputed land management activities. As we shall see, under section 13 an access authority has a duty to take steps against something which results in an obstruction or encroachment on any route, waterway or other means by which access rights may be exercised. That could include an action for interdict. An access authority does not have a more general power to vindicate access rights. That would leave matters to a member of the public, who could (for example) seek a declaration from the sheriff about whether land management is responsible under section 28, in the hope that the publicity from a court action would result in a behavioural change, or raise an action for interdict.

Duties of the landowner in relation to accessible land – Additional information

The duty of responsible land management extends to all land and inland water where access rights are not excluded. In relation to golf courses, it will be recalled that the right to cross land applies to such land (save for putting greens). Accordingly, managers of golf courses must respect that right to cross land and any unilateral steps to permanently secure the entire perimeter of a golf course, or large chunks of it, are unlikely to be classed as responsible land management.

A landowner will benefit from a presumption of responsible management when she does not cause unreasonable interference with access rights. This means *reasonable* interference will be presumed to be responsible land management. As to what reasonable interference means, any interference caused by normal outdoor activities that do not fall within the outright exclusions and taking due account of the Access Code where relevant can be regarded as reasonable. It is not irresponsible for a land manager to interfere with access rights when she has the genuine objective of preventing anticipated damage being caused to the ground by the exercise of these rights.[65] This issue will be considered below in the context of enforcement against landowners.

The Access Code is a document that land managers must pay attention to.[66] A land manager is not able to claim ignorance of its terms in order to be shielded from the regard that must be had to it.[67] It is mandatory for a court to have regard to the Code when determining if an owner has managed land responsibly, much like it is mandatory to do so when considering whether access takers have been responsible.[68]

Interestingly, unlike section 2(3) (the corresponding section for responsible access), there is no need for a landowner to take proper account of the features of the land under section 3(3). Of course, a landowner will need to consider the features of the land when seeking to minimise any potential claims under the rules relating to occupiers' liability (where the features of the land might be relevant), not to mention the features of land may lead to a designation that affects what a landowner can do,[69] but section 3(3) itself only mentions lawfulness, reasonableness, and taking proper account of the interests of others in the responsible land management mix.

Conduct excluded from responsible land management: byelaws and path reinstatement

Sections 14, 23 and possibly section 12 can operate to automatically render land management not responsible. Section 14 is considered below.

Section 12 has been discussed above in the context of byelaws for access to land. Local byelaws can also target land management. Landowners should be aware of any proposed byelaws as statutory consultees to the access authority that seeks to introduce them and should make themselves aware of existing byelaws.

Section 23 begins by declaring that nothing in the 2003 Act prevents a core path or a right of way from being ploughed or otherwise having its surface disturbed in accordance with good husbandry. It then provides that a core path or right of way that has been ploughed or otherwise disturbed must be reinstated within fourteen days or such other period as the access authority may allow, before creating the only criminal offence in this access regime of the 2003 Act. An owner who fails to reinstate a core path or right of way within fourteen days shall be guilty of an offence and liable on summary conviction to a fine (but not a custodial sentence). In those circumstances, falling short of the status of responsible land manager might not be an owner's most pressing concern, but section 3 expressly declares that such an individual cannot be taken as managing land responsibly.

Conduct excluded from responsible land management: byelaws and path reinstatement – Additional information

Section 23 replaces section 43 of the Countryside (Scotland) Act 1967, whilst introducing core paths to regulation. The offence contained in section 23(3) replaces an old offence, with the punishment of a fine not exceeding level 3 on the standard scale (at the time of writing, £1000, in terms of section 37 of the Criminal Justice Act 1982 (as amended)).

Conduct excluded from responsible land management: signs, obstructions, impediments

Section 14(1) prohibits signs, obstructions, dangerous impediments and the like that have no purpose other than restricting access rights, or in circumstances that any other purpose is so spurious or contrived as to render the associated restriction to access unjustifiable. As it is too important a provision to paraphrase, it is set out in full.

The owner of land in respect of which access rights are exercisable shall not, for the purpose or for the main purpose of preventing or deterring any person entitled to exercise these rights from doing so –

(a) put up any sign or notice;
(b) put up any fence or wall, or plant, grow or permit to grow any hedge, tree or other vegetation;
(c) position or leave at large any animal;
(d) carry out any agricultural or other operation on the land; or
(e) take, or fail to take, any other action.

The statute uses commendably understandable language here. The items listed in paragraphs (a) to (e) are largely self-explanatory, but there has still been some litigation about barriers which existed prior to the 2003 Act coming into force. Paragraphs (a) and (b) target the establishment of barriers, either by putting them up or (as regards botanical or arboreal barriers) planting them, growing them or allowing them to grow. There was a court case about a fence that was put in place prior to 2005 that suggested it and similar pre-existing barriers would probably be entitled to stay in place, but another case has since clarified that none of this should be taken as authority to keep a gate that existed in 2005 permanently locked where the gate regulates access to land on which access rights are exercisable. This is because a failure to take action (in that case, unlocking a gate) falls foul of paragraph (e). That later case has also cast doubt on the broad approach in the earlier case that pre-existing impediments to access can be allowed to remain.

Another important aspect of section 14(1) is revealed by the wording that allows a landowner to take any of the steps listed in paragraphs (a) to (e) when 'the purpose or the main purpose' of doing so is something other than preventing or deterring the exercise of access rights. This means an act or omission that is wholly or mainly targeted against access is caught, but a legitimate land management activity undertaken in accordance with the Access Code is not. That legitimate land management activity might catch some or all forms of access in the crossfire. The reciprocity of responsibility will come to the fore in such a situation: if the land management is responsible, access takers must modify their behaviour responsibly in turn.

Section 14(2) then provides that an access authority can serve a written notice on the owner of land where it considers that section 14(1) has been contravened, requiring such remedial action as is specified in the notice be taken by the owner within a specified (reasonable) timeframe. Where the owner fails to comply with such a notice, the local authority may remove the relevant sign or notice or take the remedial action specified in its written notice and recover from the owner any reasonable costs in the process. An owner can appeal this notice under section 14(4).

This has proven to be a fertile ground for litigation. It is through the operation of this section that many important clarifications have emerged, including what section 14(1) means and, in particular, what purposes are acceptable when an owner seeks to regulate access, with those purposes being assessed on an objective rather than subjective basis. That will be analysed below. The case law that has emerged has also demonstrated how important this access authority power is. Other similar powers will be considered below but it makes sense to analyse this access authority power at this stage.

Conduct excluded from responsible land management: signs, obstructions, impediments – Additional information

The case of *Aviemore Highland Resort Ltd* v *Cairngorms National Park Authority*[70] (hereafter referred to as '*Aviemore*') provides a high-profile example of pre-existing barriers being allowed to remain, so much so that it was referred to in a later case as the '*Aviemore* test' when considering similar access-restricting measures.[71] As we shall see below, that later case has now clarified that the access authority could have proceeded in a slightly different way to ensure access. The *Aviemore* case itself related to a fence which had been erected across a lane in 2004, after the 2003 Act had been passed but before it came into force (in 2005). The access authority served a section 14(2) notice about the fence. One problem for the access authority was the law which regulated new features like the fence was not in force when the fence was erected. This was characterised as a contravention of section 14(1)(b). As noted by the sheriff principal who ultimately ruled against the access authority, the prohibition targeted the putting up of a fence or wall, not (for example) the maintenance of an existing one. The section 14(2) notice accordingly failed. There was also a hedge that followed the line of the fence which section 14 might have regulated (in relation to the growing of it, rather than the planting, albeit the date of planting was not clear). The notice was not framed in a way that caught the hedge: so this issue was not tested.

The later case of *Renyana Stahl Anstalt* v *Loch Lomond and the Trossachs National Park Authority* was different, and when it was ultimately decided in the Court of Session some clarifications about *Aviemore* were offered.[72] Three gates which regulated entry to an area of land where access rights were exercisable (at Drumlean, which lies between Ben Venue and Loch Ard) were left in a default locked position by the landowner. The case was not about the erection of gates in contravention of section 14(1)(b), but rather the continuing failure of the owner to unlock them under section 14(1)(e). The case had three levels of judicial consideration, each with a slightly different result. At first instance, a sheriff ruled against the access authority. The access authority then successfully appealed to the Sheriff Appeal Court, which ordered that all three gates must be opened and (separately) the removal of a sign warning of the dangers of wild boar (as discussed below).[73] Finally, the Court of Session largely followed the Sheriff Appeal Court, with the subtle difference of only requiring two gates to be accessible (on the basis that one of the other two gates provided suitable access to the area accessible through the third gate without it being unlocked), and also not ordering the sign about boar to be taken down (as discussed below). Those subtle variations apart, the Court of Session decision essentially endorsed the practical effect of the Sheriff Appeal Court decision: namely that the land was accessible, and the landowner was correctly ordered to take steps to allow for access. The clarification that a landowner can indeed be ordered to do something when access land has been enclosed or barriered off is an important one, and the approach adopted shows why situations like the Aviemore fence might be decided differently in future. It was also made clear in the Court of Session that the proposition that seemed to flow from the sheriff principal's decision in *Aviemore* that no notice under section 14 could competently be served in respect of works, actions or omissions prior to the coming into force of the Act is 'too broadly stated'.[74]

Conduct excluded from responsible land management: signs, obstructions, impediments in action

The already mentioned *Tuley* case shows that a genuine land management decision that is not fixated on preventing or deterring access is acceptable. In that case, the landowners actually wished to facilitate many forms of access to their land in the Black Isle, but were rightly concerned about the cumulative effect of ongoing equestrian access to a particular track. They sought to close that access to horses, whilst leaving another route available for horse riders. The access authority objected to the route closure. The Court of Session ultimately ruled that the closure was permitted, as it was not wholly or mainly for the purpose of preventing or deterring access. To force landowners to thole access that was doomed to damage their land until damage occurred would not have been a fair balance.

That case can be contrasted with the more recent *Loch Lomond* case, which related to three locked gates and a sign stating 'Danger Wild Boar' at the Drumlean estate. The land manager in that case was not able to establish that the actions taken were not wholly or mainly for the purpose of preventing or deterring access. This case initially proceeded on the basis that this is to be measured *subjectively* (i.e. what did the land manager think?), an approach that both the sheriff and Sheriff Appeal Court felt they had to follow owing to comments made in the (higher ranking) Court of Session in the *Tuley* case. On further appeal to the Court of Session in the *Loch Lomond* case, it has now been clarified that the proper assessment is an *objective* one, thus rendering it unnecessary to seek to ascertain the land manager's mindset.[75] As noted above, the Court of Session did allow one of the three gates to remain locked, and also ruled the sign about boar could stay. Whilst the Sheriff Appeal Court was not convinced of the need for a sign, from the evidence it transpired a sign had actually been required by the relevant local authority in connection with an earlier boar herd.

In *Forbes* v *Fife Council* the access authority objected to landowners blocking access to a path behind their respective houses. The path was used by some access takers responsibly, but there was antisocial behaviour by others. The sheriff decided that the landowners' main purpose was to stop such antisocial (irresponsible) use of the path, which generally happened at night. The sheriff ruled that they were entitled to lock the gates overnight (between 8 p.m. and 8 a.m.). Whilst that case was decided before the Court of Session clarified that a land manager's purpose is to be assessed objectively, the case remains instructive.

Further considerations about animals, including a criminal offence of suffering or permitting any creature to cause danger or injury to any other person who is in a public place or to give such person reasonable cause for alarm or annoyance, will be considered below in the context of public rights of way.

Conduct excluded from responsible land management: signs, obstructions, impediments in action – Additional information

As noted, section 14 has proven fertile ground for litigation. In addition to the *Tuley* and *Loch Lomond* cases, the very first sheriff court case about access rights concerned the service of a section 14(2) notice at Archerfield. In *Caledonian Heritable Limited* v *East Lothian Council*[76] the access authority had served notice on the landowner relating to the erection of several signs that indicated that access was prohibited when the land (which included a golf course) was not in fact excluded from access rights. It will be recalled a golf course can be crossed under the 2003 Act, although recreational, educational or commercial activities cannot take place there.[77] The notice also related to the removal of a bridge, the erection of a barbed wire fence and the locking of gates. Despite various initial objections to the notice, the sheriff allowed the case to proceed to a proof. It later settled to the access authority's satisfaction, including the restoration of the bridge.

The *Tuley* and *Loch Lomond* cases have been discussed above. The clarification that the test to be applied in gauging whether a land manager's action or inaction was wholly or mainly for the purpose of preventing or deterring access is an objective rather than subjective one brings this aspect of the 2003 Act into line with others which are objectively assessed: for example, the extent of privacy that a homeowner/occupier can expect under section 6(1)(b)(iv).[78]

Duties of the landowner in light of the 2003 Act

As we have seen, the 2003 Act introduced a new duty on landowners to act responsibly in relation to land where access rights are exercisable, in accordance with the Access Code. This is something of an innovation when considered alongside public rights of way. As we shall see below, the traditional position is that the proprietor or occupier of the land owed limited positive duties to persons using a public right of way. That generally passive role continues where the right of way is not on land where access rights under the 2003 Act can be exercised (in terms of section 6). If the land is not excluded, it would be subject to the general duty of responsible land management.

Occupiers of land owe a duty of care to people on land and premises they have control of, both under the common law and under the Occupiers' Liability (Scotland) Act 1960. Having a duty of care means you need to take pragmatic steps to prevent harm coming someone's way, even if you have never met them before. This will be considered further in chapter 4. For present purposes it is important and interesting to note that the 2003 Act does not change this general position, by virtue of the express wording of section 5(2). Even with the potential for an increase in the number of access takers on land, there is no mitigation on this duty.

Duties of the landowner – Additional information

Section 5(2) provides, 'The extent of the duty of care owed by an occupier of land to another person present on the land is not, subject to section 22(4) below, affected by [access rights].' The exception relates to a situation when an access authority is creating or maintaining a path that it has delineated under the path order provisions in section 22 (discussed below). This was a controversial provision and it has provoked some comment.[79] It can be contrasted with the position in England and Wales under its statutory access regime.[80] The law of delict generally, and occupiers' liability in particular, are specialist areas and it is not possible to cover them fully in this guide. Some outline coverage is provided in chapter 4.

Duties and powers of access authorities

Local authorities and, where relevant, national park authorities play an important role in the scheme of the 2003 Act. They have extensive duties and powers in relation to the access rights. Where a duty exists, the access authority *must* act. Where a power exists, the access authority *may* act. This means there is a discretion in relation to the use of powers, subject to the usual controls of administrative law (particularly judicial review, which might be appropriate in relation to a manifestly unjustifiable decision or non-decision).

Duties of access authorities

Access authorities have the duty to:

(i) uphold statutory access rights (section 13);

(ii) keep core paths plans, any maps they refers to and a list of core paths available for public inspection and for sale at a reasonable price (section 18(8)), which builds on the initial duty on each access authority to draw up and adopt a plan sufficient for the purpose of giving the public reasonable access throughout their area (sections 17–18), and to review its system of core paths when required by Ministers (section 20), which can be thought of as the continuing core path duty;

(iii) work with local access forums when exercising its powers to exempt particular land, proposing byelaws and reviewing its core paths, which follows on from the duty to establish local access forums in each access authority area (section 25); and

(iv) have regard to guidance issued by the Scottish Ministers on the performance of any of its functions (section 27).

Core paths and local access forums will be discussed further below.

Duties of access authorities – Additional information

The duty in section 13 sets up the relevant access authority as the access champion for the area, although it must be noted that the duty is not to uphold access rights in general. The duty operates within certain parameters, namely the access authority must 'assert, protect and keep open and free from obstruction or encroachment any route, waterway or other means by which access rights may reasonably be exercised'.[81] It operates alongside an equivalent function for rights of way. The duty in relation to access rights is not limited to core paths, although in practice access authorities may prioritise resources to them.

In relation to core paths themselves, the initial duty to draw up a network of core paths, within three years of the 2003 Act coming into force, has now been fulfilled by all access authorities. Over and above the duty to keep core paths plans available for public inspection and for sale at a reasonable price, they also have a continuing role in relation to core paths, but that can only be properly classed as a duty in a situation when Scottish Ministers ask for a core paths plan to be reviewed.

The duty to work with local access forums only operates in tandem with the exercise of other access authority powers. Local access forums had an important role in the introduction of core paths. Their three mandated roles as consultees are now found in section 11 (suspension of access rights), section 12 (byelaws) and section 20 (review and amendment of a core paths plan). Its more general continuing role is to offer and, where the offer is accepted, to give assistance to the parties to any dispute about the exercise of access rights, the existence and delineation of rights of way and the use of core paths. An access authority is not obliged to accept an offer of advice or to do anything with any advice that is accepted in relation to this more general role, but it might be hoped the insight of a representative local access forum would be afforded due respect.

Guidance can be issued under section 27 either generally or in relation to a specific access authority. The general guidance issued by Scottish Ministers has been referred to above.

Powers of access authorities

Access authorities have powers to:

(i)   institute and defend legal proceedings relative to the duty to uphold access rights (section 13(3));

(ii) deal with obstructions, dangerous impediments and signs on all access land (and public rights of way) (section 14);

(iii) carry out measures on all access land (and public rights of way) for safety, protection, guidance and assistance, which may include the erection and maintenance of signs and notices, the installation of gates, stiles, moorings, launching sites or similar, and dealing with electric fences and barbed wire (section 15);

(iv) acquire land to enable or facilitate exercise of access rights (section 16);

(v)   maintain core paths (section 19);

  (vi) review its system of core paths at such time as they consider appropriate (section 20, with the process for doing so in sections 20A–20D);

 (vii) enter into path agreements (section 21);

(viii) delineate paths by path orders (section 22);

  (ix) order reinstatement of core paths (and public rights of way) after ploughing and, if relevant, take steps to reinstate the path (section 23);

   (x) appoint rangers in relation to any land in respect of which access rights are exercisable (section 24); and

  (xi) enter land for a purpose connected with their functions under Part 1 of the 2003 Act (section 26).

The operation of section 14 has been illustrated above and highlights situations where an access authority has acted in the past. Accordingly, only brief additional coverage of it is provided below.

By virtue of section 31, sections 14 and 15 also apply in relation to rights of way by foot, horseback, pedal cycle or any combination of those as they apply in relation to access rights.

Not much needs to be said here about section 16. This allows the acquisition of land to take place to facilitate access rights, which might be appropriate for the acquisition of a car park near a beauty spot. It follows a recognised statutory process and formula for compulsory purchase. The other powers are analysed individually.

These powers and the earlier duties are all found in Chapter 5 of Part 1 of the 2003 Act, which is entitled 'Local authority functions: access and other rights'. Of the sections in that chapter that have not been listed above, sections 17 and 18 related to the creation of core paths. As these have now been introduced, it is not necessary to set out the powers or the processes used when they were introduced. Their effect and the potential to amend a core paths plan will, however, be analysed below.

Similarly, section 25 related to the creation of local access forums. Now that these are in force, it is more important to focus on the roles they play than their creation. Their role has been considered above and will be further explained below.

Powers of access authorities – Additional information

In terms of when an access authority should act under section 14, The Scottish Government's guidance gives the following examples of types of action which, if deliberately used to prevent or deter the public from exercising their access rights, would justify an access authority using its statutory powers to intervene:

- Erecting signs or notices which deter the public from entering land over which access rights are exercisable;
- Erecting fences or walls or planting hedges, trees or other vegetation;
- Blocking culverts;
- Leaving any animal of a type which could be considered to have a dangerous propensity in a field crossed by a core path;
- Parking vehicles, trailers, equipment, building or fencing materials in such a way as to unreasonably impede access;
- Storing or depositing dung, straw, or any animal food stuffs on a path, road or gateway so as to unreasonably impede access;
- Locking gates.

Measures for safety, protection, guidance and assistance

An access authority is empowered to take such steps as it thinks appropriate to warn the public of and protect the public from danger on any land in respect of which access rights are exercisable, including putting up and maintaining notices and fences. They can do this without prior authorisation of the owner. They can also, with the consent of the owner, install access easing features such as gates, stiles, moorings and launching sites, and provide staff or apparatus to help protect life in relation to accessible inland water. (Mooring equipment that is installed without a landowner's permission is vulnerable to removal.)[82]

Sections 15(2) and 15(3) apply the section 14 enforcement regime to a fence, wall or other erection that has been constructed or adapted (whether by the use of barbed wire or other sharp material or by being electrified or otherwise) in a way that is likely to injure a person exercising access rights, allowing an access authority to act against these.

Core paths

The 2003 Act introduced a framework for a new system of paths, called 'core paths', to provide the public with reasonable access throughout each access authority area. In the years which followed the 2003 Act coming into force, each access authority designed and implemented a core paths plan, with input from relevant stakeholders. Core paths are not intended to meet all path needs, but they serve an important role in the tapestry of access provision. Core paths plans were designed to meet existing and future needs of different categories of users, such as walkers and horse-riders, including all-ability paths. Where access needs have changed, an access authority can change its core paths plan by following the statutory procedure, again with the input of interested parties.

Much of this is a matter for access authorities. It is still important for access takers to know how core paths work, to ensure the proper use of them and to hold landowners and access authorities to account. As regards the former, an access taker can generally be confident that access rights will apply on a core path, unless there are extraordinary circumstances such as an outbreak of animal illness or a specific suspension of them by an access authority acting under section 11. An access authority, as noted above (page 77), has certain powers regarding a core path, such as in relation to its reinstatement after it has been ploughed or otherwise disturbed by a landowner, or maintenance more generally.

The Guidance published by the Scottish Executive (as the Scottish Government was then known) in 2005 stated that core paths plans normally comprise three elements: a map or maps of the core paths system; a list of designated core paths; and any relevant supporting text. Designated core paths should be shown clearly on the published maps, which should also illustrate the context of (for example) links to other paths, minor roads, public transport and recreational sites. Like public rights of way (discussed below in chapter 3), core paths are not displayed on the official Ordnance Survey map, although a case can be made for this, as discussed on page 129 below. Scottish Natural Heritage has created a website that shows all the core paths in Scotland on a single interactive map (www.nature.scot/enjoying-outdoors/places-visit/routes-explore/local-path-networks).

Core paths – Additional information

Sections 17 and 18 of the 2003 Act were crucial in the introduction of the core paths network but they are now largely of historic interest. They do, however, hook into the process that an access authority must follow if and when it reviews and amends its core paths plan.

Section 18(8) obliged an access authority to give public notice of the adoption of a core paths plan, and to compile a list of core paths, and obliges it to keep its core paths plan available for public inspection and for sale at a reasonable price.

Section 20 deals with the review and amendment of a core paths plan. It was amended and supplemented by the Land Reform (Scotland) Act 2016, which introduced further procedure when making amendments. A review *must* be made if required by Ministers or *may* be made if the access authority considers it appropriate to do so for the purpose of ensuring that the core paths plan continues to give the public reasonable access throughout their area.

There are slightly different regimes for removing or diverting a core path as compared to introducing a new path. An access authority may not remove or divert a path[83] unless it satisfied that it is expedient so to do having regard to (a) the extent to which it appears to them that persons would, but for the amendment, be likely to exercise access rights using the core path; and (b) the effect which the amendment of the plan would have as respects land served by the core path. An access authority is obliged to update its list of core paths to show the effect of any stopping up or diversion (by order under section 208 of the Town and Country Planning (Scotland) Act 1997) and thereafter to keep its amended plan available for public inspection and for sale. It must be remembered that using any of these powers to change a core path will not change any right of way that exists along the same alignment.[84] Separate powers exist in relation to rights of way, as discussed in chapter 3.

As regards an amendment that brings in a new path, sections 17(3) and 17(4) are applied to set out the criteria to which the access authority should have regard in drawing up a new plan, and sections 20A–20C set out the procedure for public consultation, landowner notification and adoption of the plan. An amended core paths plan and related maps must be made available for review for 12 weeks, allowing for comparison with the previous plan, and consultation with interested parties, such as Scottish Natural Heritage, the local access forum and representative persons. As with section 18, which set out the regime which applied when core paths were introduced, landowners are not explicitly mentioned amongst the consultees, but they are indirectly and directly provided for by other means. Representatives of them will invariably be amongst those listed in section 20A(1)(c) (namely those who live, work, carry on business or engage in recreational activities on the land affected by the amendment) giving them a potential role in a consultation. Moreover, and in contrast to the original scheme of section 18, owners and occupiers of land that is to be included in a plan for the first time must be notified of this in accordance with section 20B. If an objection is made, an access authority must not adopt the amended plan unless Scottish Ministers direct them to do so. There is provision for a local inquiry to be held if an objection is not withdrawn. The various permutations of this process will not be considered in this guide. On the assumption that the plan is eventually adopted, the access authority must publicise the amended plan and make it available for public inspection and for sale at a reasonable price.

For a minor amendment to a core paths plan, section 20C provides that an access authority may make a single amendment without instigating a full plan review where the access authority considers this would be appropriate. The flexibility afforded to a local authority for this exercise seems striking in comparison to a full review, in that it can consult and notify as it thinks fit in a period it specifies, although section 20D makes clear that a local authority is still subject to a defined procedure.

Section 19 is important for core paths 'on the ground', dealing as it does with maintenance, enabling the flow of access takers, and provision of directions to and information about core paths. Significantly, the access authority is not obliged to maintain core paths or direct the public to them; it only has the power to do so.

Delineation of access land: path agreements and path orders

There are two sections in the 2003 Act which provide for delineation of paths where access rights are exercisable. Section 21 is to be used where the access authority and the landowner are in agreement, while section 22 can be used by the access authority without the agreement of the landowner: that is to say, it is a form of compulsion.

Section 21 is non-controversial. It provides that the access authority may enter into path agreement for the delineation, creation (if relevant), and maintenance of a path in respect of which access rights are exercisable. That path agreement may be on such terms and conditions as to payment as are agreed.

Section 22 carries more clout than section 21. It can apply where it is impracticable to secure a path agreement, but if the access authority (having regard to the rights and interests of the landowner and potential access takers) is of the view it is expedient to delineate a path within that land, the authority may, by order, do so. Such an order is called a path order. This power has only been used once since the 2003 Act came into force.

Delineation of access land: path agreements and path orders – Additional information

The power to delineate/create a path for use by the public by agreement or by order largely supersedes similar powers contained in sections 30 and 31 of the Countryside (Scotland) Act 1967 respectively, although those powers were not fully repealed, to allow them to continue in respect of land which is excluded under the 2003 Act and in relation to any rights and facilities afforded to the public under those sections which are not secured by the 2003 Act.

Path orders can only be made if the procedure in schedule 1 of the 2003 Act is followed. This requires notice to be given to the landowner. The landowner can object, and if she does the Scottish Ministers must confirm the path order before it can have effect. On exercising this power, depending on whether there is a path physically in existence on the ground, the access authority will then either have a duty to simply maintain an existing path or have a duty to create and maintain a path. Those duties are relevant in determining whether a local authority has control of a path for the purposes of the Occupiers' Liability (Scotland) Act 1960. All of this means that an access authority must consider carefully whether these powers are appropriate. A path order must contain a map showing the delineation of the path and must comply with a prescribed template.[85]

Particulars of a path order are to be entered into the burdens section of a title sheet in accordance with section 9(1)(e) of the Land Registration etc. (Scotland) Act 2012 (asp 5). Path orders are also relevant to other aspects of land registration practice: e.g. under section 73 of that Act, the Keeper of the Registers of Scotland offers no warranty that land is unencumbered by a path delineated under section 22 of the Land Reform (Scotland) Act 2003.

Rangers and their powers of entry

Under section 24, rangers can be appointed by an access authority to advise and assist the owner of the land and other members of the public as to any matter relating to the exercise of access rights in respect of the land and to perform such other duties in relation to the exercise of access rights as the access authority thinks appropriate. To that end, rangers have a statutory power to enter any land in respect of which access rights are exercisable, without notice, in order to exercise their functions.

Access authorities: powers of entry

Access authorities have a power of entry, under section 26, to enter *any* land for a purpose connected with the exercise or proposed exercise of any of the access authority's functions under the 2003 Act, but only at a reasonable time and on giving reasonable notice to the owner of the land, unless there is an emergency or when entry is needed for safety or maintenance purposes relating to a core path.

Court actions relating to access rights

As we have seen, one route to court is where a landowner appeals against a notice served by an access authority under section 14 of the 2003 Act. The route to court that is not predicated on an access authority taking action is provided by section 28 of the 2003 Act. This empowers a sheriff to declare whether land is subject to access rights and whether a person exercising access rights or managing land has done so responsibly, when someone makes a summary application. The proceedings take the form of an application for a 'declarator': that is to say, for the court to declare something. The section does not provide for the imposition of penalties in the event of behaviour being declared as irresponsible. When determining if someone has acted responsibly, the sheriff will look to section 2 (responsible access) and section 3 (responsible management) and, if relevant, apply the presumption of responsible conduct to anyone not causing unreasonable interference in the terms of the 2003 Act.

The powers and duties of local authorities relative to court proceedings in relation to statutory access rights have already been noted above. It should also be noted that, as the rights are available to 'everyone', this means everyone has title to raise court proceedings. That is not to say, however, that there could not be an extreme case where proceedings have been raised maliciously and where the court might hold that someone had no genuine interest to enforce the action. Such a case would be unusual but it might occur if proceedings were raised merely as another device to assist an individual locked in a boundary dispute with his neighbour.

It can be questioned whether the 2003 Act allows for an accessible dispute resolution procedure when dealing with questions about responsible access. On encountering irresponsible access, there is little option between the extremes of solving a problem independently (which might not be suitable or safe in all circumstances) and referring a matter to the sheriff. The practicalities and expense of raising such an action means that it is unlikely anything other extreme cases of irresponsible access or competing activities when money-making is at stake will result in a sheriff court ruling. The one other statutory option available before an application to the sheriff involves a local access forum. Local access forums can offer assistance to the parties of any dispute, but cannot offer a ruling. This lack of an accessible means to resolve low or mid level access disputes has the potential to leave them festering at a local level. Reform in this area would be welcome.

Court actions relating to access rights – Additional Information

The question of who will or may be involved with such an action, depends on who raises it. If it is the landowner (which would normally be the case when seeking a declaration that land is excluded from access rights), the landowner must serve notice of the application on the access authority and, if relevant, any person who the landowner claims is not acting responsibly.[86] For anyone else, the person raising the action must serve the application on the landowner, and the relevant access authority (which has a statutory right to be a party to proceedings).[87] It is also possible for interested groups to intervene in proceedings under section 28, as happened in the *Gloag* case with Ramblers Scotland.

The guidance in the Access Code on what to do when irresponsible behaviour is encountered can be distilled to: ask the access taker to modify his behaviour; contact the police if what he is doing is criminal; never use force; and be prepared to refer the matter to the sheriff.[88] That plan of action is generally sensible, although it (a) presupposes people will know what is responsible, and (b) leaves the only means to determine that question with a sheriff.

As noted, this dispute resolution deficit can be, and has been, criticised.[89] Whilst giving the modern access regime a stamp of approval, the Final Report of the Land Reform Review Group suggested an alternative form of dispute resolution might be appropriate, such as making more use of dispute resolution techniques such as mediation and arbitration.[90] An access tribunal has also been suggested.[91] The writer proposed an alternative form of dispute resolution, suggesting local access forums could play a role, particularly in relation to access takers in dispute with each other.[92] For this, local access forums could become a first-instance decision maker, putting them into a mediation/arbitration role rather than a non-binding conciliation/mediation role. That could only happen alongside a consideration of (for example) the appointments to a local access forum. There are pros and cons to each of these suggestions, but it is submitted that any streamlined process, interposed between current non-binding processes and a judicial determination, could allow disputes to be resolved without the need for a court action. Prior to the enactment of the Land Reform (Scotland) Act 2016, the Scottish Parliament's Rural Affairs, Climate Change and Environment Committee recommended that the author's proposal be taken forward to allow local access forums to deal with minor access rights disputes.[93] This did not find its way into the 2016 Act.

Reciprocal responsibilities: what all of this means for the access taker

Now that we have considered access rights in full, and in particular where and how they can be exercised, and how those exercising rights interact with each other, it might be helpful to reflect on what all this means for someone interested in taking access to land and intent on being responsible when doing so. In this exercise, a rough hierarchy of whose conduct an access taker needs to show deference to begins to emerge. To a certain extent, this straddles the 'where' and 'how' divide, of excluded *places* and excluded/responsible *conduct*, but those two questions of 'where' and 'how' can still usefully be at the forefront of any access taker's mind when considering where or what is allowed.

It will be recalled that a person is presumed to be exercising access rights responsibly if they are exercised so as to not cause unreasonable interference with any of the rights of any other person. Those rights could be access rights, rights associated with the ownership of land, or any others. It will also be recalled there are some activities which can never be classed as responsible access (such as hunting, shooting and fishing).

To be safely classed as responsible, an access taker should therefore not do any such excluded activity and should strive not to interfere with the day-to-day activities of others. When exercising a statutory access right, one should have regard to the interests of the occupier of the land as, for example, an agriculturalist, forester or sportsman. (This also applies, as a matter of courtesy, when using a right of way.) This is especially true of the lambing season and of the game shooting and deer stalking seasons. If unreasonable interference with others takes place, the presumption of responsible access no longer applies.

In law, that is not actually the end of the assessment exercise of what is responsible, it would just mean the access taker no longer benefits from the presumption. It would still be theoretically possible for an access taker to be classed as taking access responsibly if the access rights were being exercised in a lawful and reasonable manner that took proper account of the interests of others and the features of the land in question (in accordance with section 2(3) of the 2003 Act).

Looking at each of these in turn, any activity which breaches the criminal law cannot be a responsible exercise of access rights. Next, exercise of the rights must be reasonable. This is not defined, although logically it will mean that obstinately adopting a course of action without modifying behaviour when faced with fair instructions or a change in circumstances will not be reasonable. Taking proper account of the features of the land will be context specific. Not doing so might involve a whole manner of activities that damage land or the capability of land to support certain flora or fauna in a way that falls short of a criminal offence. Finally, taking into account the interests of others offers the chance to thoroughly revisit the issues which would have been raised when assessing that the access taker should not benefit from the aforementioned presumption of responsible access.

With this in mind, the following places and personalities must be considered, and in many cases deferred, to by an access taker ('X'), in accordance with the following hierarchy.

(1) **Excluded land:** in access rights terms, X must show complete deference to the owner and those deriving rights from the owner or who have other rights (see 3 below). X has no legal entitlement to be there at all without permission unless there is another right, such as a public right of way. X must also defer to an owner's requirements to abstain from particular conduct on excluded land. However, where the exclusion is a periodic one that is tied to use (such as a playing field), the exclusion will not apply when the land is not being so used.

(2) **Responsible management on non-excluded land:** deference must be shown to an owner, or those deriving rights from the owner, engaging in a responsible programme of land management which takes due account of the Access Code.

(3) **Other non-2003 Act parties:** deference must be shown to a person who has a specific right to engage in a particular activity on the land when that person is undertaking that activity, where that entitlement is connected to neither ownership nor the 2003 Act (such as a statutory undertaker, as would be the case with installation and maintenance of electricity pylons).

(4) **Other 2003 Act parties on land responsibly set aside for their particular use:** deference should be shown to another access taker engaging in any activity in a zone where that particular conduct is contemplated in a manner that would be classed as responsible access, where X is not also engaging in similar conduct (for example, X walks across a ski-slope, where another access taker is skiing).

(5) **Other access takers with no innate priority:** proper consideration should be taken of other access takers engaging in any activity that would be classed as responsible access:

    (a) in a zone where that particular conduct is contemplated and where X is also engaging in similar conduct; *or*

    (b) on land not necessarily associated with any particular conduct.

In terms of the interaction between access takers in situation 4, X would be hard pressed to prove he is being responsible if his pedestrian access is getting in the way of (say) equestrian access in an area the landowner has steered horses to. Meanwhile, a skier who goes off-piste may struggle to prove she has been responsible in a dispute with a non-skiing access taker who judiciously avoided a recognised ski-slope.

In situation 5 (a), both access takers may be entitled to be on the land, and may be undertaking a particular responsible activity, but they still need to be considerate of one another, e.g. cyclists slowing down when passing one another on a route used for mountain biking. As for 5 (b), the setting for such interaction might be a grass football pitch within a public park that is not being used for football, where one group had planned to throw a frisbee but on arrival another group is playing rounders. It would not be responsible access for the later arriving group to seek to usurp the earlier group, but in turn the earlier group would not be responsible if they extended their activity purely to deny access to others.

It is stressed that the competition is only framed from the perspective of the access taker; from other perspectives different results could ensue. For example, there may be times when an owner must tolerate another party's rights, such as a right of way or traditional rights of access for fishing, unless the owner somehow manages to reassert a clean title, say by the loss of a public right of way by negative prescription. The hierarchy also makes no mention of emergency services, which would expect to be able to perform their roles without disturbance by an access taker, or an access authority, which may be able to interpose itself in the hierarchy in a variety of situations to fulfil its statutory functions, or an access authority's rangers.

Reciprocal responsibilities: what all of this means for the access taker – Additional information

This hierarchy is modelled on that proposed in the 2014 article 'Get off that land: non-owner regulation of access to land'.[94]

It can be noted that an access taker might begin a journey or activity in one category then migrate to another, perhaps on deciding to set up camp next to a right of way. This could be an acceptable use of access rights, but camping on the right of way, in such a way as to block it, would not be, as it would interfere with the rights of others, and it could even be a criminal offence in some circumstances.[95] This leads to another disclaimer, namely that access takers are always subject to the controls of criminal law or any other automatically imposed private law obligations. Regarding the latter, much in the same way as a landowner cannot escape the rules of occupiers' liability simply because of the existence of access rights, neither can an access taker escape the underlying law of delict. In particular, the law of nuisance (which is normally relevant to objectionable use of land by the owner) could apply to restrict obnoxious behaviour by an individual on someone else's land.

The logic for placing 3 (other rights holders) before 4 and 5 (other access takers) is that non-2003 Act rights of access are not subject to the additional requirement that such rights are exercised responsibly or coupled with a statutory encouragement not to unreasonably interfere with any rights of anyone else.

Conclusion

This chapter has set out the role and place of access rights under the 2003 Act in modern Scots law. There is no indication that this role will diminish, which can be demonstrated in part by the fact the Scottish Parliament declined the opportunity to radically reform them when it passed the Land Reform (Scotland) Act 2016. That important role notwithstanding, as this and the preceding chapter of this guide have made clear, there are other important aspects of Scots law that regulate access. These will be considered in the rest of this guide.

3
Rights of Way and Other Public Access

'The existence or exercise of access rights does not diminish or displace any other rights (whether public or private) of entry, way, passage or access.' So proclaims section 5(3) of the 2003 Act. Similarly, section 5(4) notes 'any public rights under the guardianship of the Crown in relation to the foreshore' are not diminished or displaced. These rights accordingly continue.

This prompts several questions. What is a public right of way? How is one created? What are you entitled to do on one, and how may you do that?

A brief definition of a public right of way is a right of passage from a place where the public are entitled to be to a place where the public are entitled to be.[1] This definition and the other issues raised will be analysed further below, as will the related sub-question of what makes a public place and the standalone topics of access to the foreshore and access to rivers. Before doing so, some further introductory remarks are necessary to put this in context following on from the discussion in chapter 2.

The access rights that we learned of in chapter 2 of this guide can co-exist in relation to areas where other rights of access subsist, because access rights apply to all land unless it is excluded, and land that is traversed by a public right of way is not one of the listed exclusions. Meanwhile, in the 2003 Act land is defined as including the foreshore, under section 32, and a separate (overlapping) access regime applies there.

It is necessary to make two observations in light of this. The first is one that has been alluded to several times in this guide already, namely that land traversed by a public right of way (or indeed the foreshore) might be excluded from access rights for one of the reasons listed in section 6, hence the continuing need for such rights and hence the need for the provisions in section 5 declaring their continuing existence. Meanwhile, despite the wide range of activities allowed under the 2003 Act, access rights cannot be used for motorised access, except in the case of a vehicle that aids mobility in appropriate circumstances. A public right of way may be vehicular.

The second observation is from a slightly different perspective, namely what happens when the rights overlap and co-exist. At the outset of this chapter what the public can do on a right of way is explained. The activities listed will be the limits of what they can do on the land *as a right of way*, but where access rights are not excluded a member of the public will also be able to (responsibly) cross and be on that land under the 2003 Act, provided no interference with those using the right of way takes place. Rather than give this disclaimer every time, that should be taken as a given throughout this chapter, allowing rights of way to be focussed on without distraction by access rights unless it is particularly useful to highlight them.

That differentiates access rights and public rights of way. A further differentiation, highlighted in chapter 1, is between public and private rights of access. The latter are servitudes, which have their own rules. Of course, there are also some similarities, not least the fact they both allow people to travel from one place to elsewhere, and some cases relating to one classification can be used by analogy with another, but before proceeding on our journey through rights of way it would be useful to reiterate or introduce some important differences between public rights of way and servitudes.

The first is that public rights of way can be used by anyone, whereas servitudes can be used only by the proprietor of land that benefits from the servitude right or a narrow class of related individuals (such as a tenant). That leads to a related observation: a servitude requires there to be a burdened property (that being the plot of land the route traverses) and at least one benefited property. There is, however, no need for a benefited property for a public right of way: in other words, there is only a burdened property. Meanwhile, a servitude of access can, and in most cases will, facilitate access to private land, but a public right of way must connect two public places. Finally, servitudes can allow the use of land for purposes such as laying pipes. A public right of way is for passage only.

What activity can the public carry out?

A public right of way is a right of passage, and passage only. The means by which passage can be taken will depend on the nature of the right of way. The nature of the right of way will in turn depend on how the right of way comes into existence, during which process it will normally be necessary to provide evidence of its use for passage from one end to the other over a period of twenty years. All of this will be discussed below. Where the nature of the right of way limits the means by which passage can be taken, that does not prevent responsible access being taken where the 2003 Act applies, under that regime.

Once a route has been established as a public right of way, a person may use part of it only, or use the public right of way to obtain access to immediately adjacent land owned by him, with reference to the cases of *McRobert* v *Reid*[2] and *Lord Burton* v *Mackay*.[3]

What activity can the public carry out? – Additional information

A public right of way gives no right to camp, hunt, shoot or fish, it gives a right of passage only.[4] As noted at the outset of this chapter, access rights may allow some activities that cannot normally be derived from a right of way. From the example activities given, this could allow e.g. camping, but not hunting, shooting or fishing as they are excluded from responsible conduct under section 9 of the 2003 Act.

Different uses of rights of way

In Scots law, in contrast with certain legal systems, there is no hard and fast classification of different types of public rights of way (as explained by Rankine, an important writer on Scottish land law).[5] It is still usual and useful to distinguish between public rights of way on foot (for pedestrians), on horseback (with routes for horse riders known as bridle paths), or in carts or carriages (a categorisation that now includes motor vehicles). It may be emphasised, to adapt words used by Lord President Clyde in the case of *Carstairs* v *Spence*,[6] 'that the prescriptive use of a right of way not merely establishes the existence of the right but, in an important way, defines the extent of the right'. As a result, proof of a right to use the route for vehicular traffic would include the various lesser rights to use the route for the traffic of persons on horseback or on foot.

The converse is not true and the fact that a route is a pedestrian public right of way does not, it is thought, permit its use by persons on horseback or in or on vehicles. There is one exception to this: it has been held that a public right of way originally established through use by horse drawn carts and carriages gives a right to its use by motor cars, at least where the right was originally created at a date when such horse drawn carts were the primary form of traffic now replaced by cars.[7] Exactly how far this exception can be stretched to include heavy commercial vehicles, or vehicles fitted with tracks, such as tanks, or vehicles of the 'hovercraft' type, is open to question. It is thought that motor cycles would be assimilated to motor cars in this context.

Creation of rights of way will be considered below, but for now it can be noted that a right of way created by deed might be treated differently. It appears possible to use a deed to create a right of access for vehicles only, not including pedestrians, in a situation where access by pedestrians might be dangerous or otherwise unsuitable (subject to any other rights people might have to be on such a route, including under the 2003 Act).

It should be emphasised that people on rights of way, such as cyclists and horse riders, must use them with due consideration for the rights of other users. A person who drives furiously or recklessly a horse or other animal on a road (a term inclusive of pedestrian rights of way) commits an offence under section 129(7) of the Roads (Scotland) Act 1984. Similarly, a person who rides a cycle on a road recklessly or without due care and attention is guilty of an offence (under sections 28 and 29 of the Road Traffic Act 1988). There is also a common law charge of reckless or furious driving of a vehicle or riding of a cycle, already highlighted in chapter 2. Pedal cycles will be considered in more detail below. As for pedestrians, it is an offence under section 53 of the Civic Government (Scotland) Act 1982 to wilfully obstruct any other person's lawful passage in a public place.

It can also be an offence under section 53 to simply obstruct lawful passage in a public place (that is to say, the obstruction does not need to be wilful) where that obstruction takes place with at least one other person and also where a person causing an obstruction does not desist on being required to do so by a constable in uniform.

Reference should also be made to section 129(5) of the Roads (Scotland) Act 1984. This states that, unless there is some other specific right, it is an offence to ride or propel a vehicle (a term which includes a bicycle) on a footway or footpath unless it is also a cycle track, and also that it is an offence to ride a horse on a footway, footpath or cycle path. It is submitted that the right of responsible access under the 2003 Act, discussed in the previous chapter, could be such a specific right and as such there will be no offence in situations of responsible access, but the interaction of these two legislative regimes could be clearer.

Different uses of rights of way – Additional information

As noted, there is no strict categorisation of different types of public rights of way, but they can be roughly be compared with English rights of way as follows: pedestrian rights of way are akin to English footpaths, bridle paths for horses to English bridleways, and vehicular rights of ways to byways.

The principle that authorisation of an onerous form of access includes a lesser form of access is well known. This would mean a bridle path could be used by pedestrians.[8] For the converse not being true, and pedestrian usage not giving rise to a vehicular route, see *Cuthbertson* v *Young*[9] and *Jenkins* v *Murray*.[10]

Pedal cycles and other forms of self-propulsion

The question of how to treat pedal cycles is an interesting one. Are they vehicles or are they extensions of the pedestrian's power to walk? There is one important reported case in relation of public rights of way and pedal cycles: *Aberdeenshire County Council* v *Lord Glentanar*,[11] sometimes called the Glentanar right of way case. It seems possible that the use of pedal cycles over a route for the prescriptive period subject to the usual conditions for the establishment of a public right of way would create for them a public right of way. Cyclists may also use a carriage road and, possibly, a bridle path subject, of course, to any express exclusion in the terms of an express grant if that is how the right of access has been constituted. It is not clear, however, that pedal cycles may be used on a route which is (merely) a pedestrian public right of way. As noted above, it is an offence to ride or propel a vehicle, a term which includes a bicycle, on a footway or footpath unless it is also a cycle track, or there is some other specific right. It is submitted that the right of responsible access under the 2003 Act, discussed in the previous chapter, could be such a specific right in situations where access is responsible. As regards non-criminal aspects of the underlying right reference can be made to the judgment of Lord Mackay in the aforementioned Glentanar right of way case, where he differentiated between devices with some form of motive power or something that channels an individual's energy to travel more quickly. That case settled before a definitive pronouncement could be made on the issue.

Pedal cycles and other forms of self-propulsion – Additional information

In the Glentanar right of way case, Lord Mackay distinguished between machines which had some form of motive power and 'on the other hand, any form of contrivance, such as a skate or roller skate or ski or snow shoe, which merely facilitates the use of the individual's own muscle to cover the ground more quickly.'[12] This judgment, however, was reclaimed (or appealed) to the Inner House of the Court of Session and the case was eventually settled by an agreement which was ratified by that Court on 10th December 1931. The Inner House, therefore, had no opportunity to consider Lord Mackay's views on the matter.

The offence of riding or propelling a vehicle (a term which includes a bicycle) on a footway or footpath unless it is also a cycle track is found in the Roads (Scotland) Act 1984, section 129(5). This provision does not apply to prams, push chairs and invalid carriages.

Where?

A public right of way normally follows a specific track, path or road on the surface of the land, but in open country it is not essential that there should be a visible track.[13] There is no reason in principle why a public right of way may not be established over an artificial structure, such as a bridge.[14] Public rights of way traditionally were limited to activities on the surface of land and were not developed to deal with activities such as paragliding or potholing.

The user of the public right of way must follow its general line unless there is some natural obstruction, such as a landslide or flooding. Otherwise, there is no inherent right to divert from the route of the public right of way on to other parts of the owner's land. Ordnance Survey maps will show tracks, but in Scotland, there is always a note on such maps indicating that the mere existence of a track is not evidence of a public right of way. Information about public rights of way and paths or routes which may be rights of way can be obtained from most access authorities, or from ScotWays, which maintains the National Catalogue of Rights of Way (CROW). No access authority has power to declare any track or route as a public right of way: that is a matter for the courts alone.

The statutory definition of road, incorporating public rights of way

Although the primary source of law relating to rights of way in Scotland is still the common law, in recent times there has been an increasing amount of statutory intervention. Statutory provisions have not always tracked the language of the common law, which means it is necessary to consider some important definitions.

A public right of way comes within the definition of the term 'road' in section 151 of the Roads (Scotland) Act 1984 ('the 1984 Act'). It provides that 'road' means:

> any way (other than a waterway) over which there is a public right of passage (by whatever means) and whether subject to a toll or not and includes the road's verge, and any bridge

(whether permanent or temporary) over which, or tunnel through which, the road passes. . .

Statutory access rights do not constitute a public right of passage for the purposes of this definition, in terms of section 5(6) of the 2003 Act. For present purposes, this means regulatory rules that have no impact on access rights are relevant to public rights of way. Relatedly, the definition of 'road' has been incorporated by reference into other statutes.[15]

Under the 1984 Act a 'public road' means one which a roads authority has a duty to maintain and a 'private road' is one where it has no such duty. It follows that most cross country public rights of way come within the definition of 'private road'. If a public road loses that status (by virtue of its deletion from the list of public roads by the relevant authority), that has no impact on the public right of way.[16] It may be added that a 'footway' is one which is associated with a carriage way and that a 'footpath' is one which is not so associated. A footpath is defined in section 47 the 1967 Act as 'a way over which the public have the following, but no other, rights of way, that is to say, a right of way on foot with or without a right of way on pedal cycles'.

The statutory definition of road, incorporating public rights of way – Additional information

For a time, it was unclear how the expression used in the 1984 Act – 'public right of passage (by whatever means)' – interacted with the already established terminology of 'public right of way'. This was clarified in the case of *Hamilton* v *Dumfries and Galloway Council (No. 2)*,[17] which made clear that the language of the 1984 Act did not create a new conceptually distinct public right of passage. In that case, it was unsuccessfully argued that a public right of passage could have survived a stopping up order that targeted what had been a section of the B724 road. (The old road had become surplus to requirements owing to the construction of a new bypass and related road diversions.) This decision had the effect of preventing the (re)adoption of the stopped up road by the relevant local authority, as the subsequent use since the stopping up had not been sufficient to constitute a public right of way.

Local authorities and public rights of way

The role of local authorities as regards public rights of way is not as easily summarised as the equivalent role under the 2003 Act. Planning authorities have important duties in the context of public rights of way, but it is hardly practicable in the course of this short guide to specify their precise allocation. Some relevant duties will be highlighted, including the important duty contained in section 46 of the 1967 Act. It provides:

> It shall be the duty of a ... planning authority to assert, protect, and keep open and free from obstruction or encroachment any public right of way which is wholly or partly within their area, and they may for these purposes institute and defend legal proceedings and generally take such steps as they may deem expedient.

Some local authorities have construed the term 'assert' as implying more than an 'informal assertion' to concerned persons, or a formal assertion, by taking legal proceedings. They have in some cases set up administrative procedures for the assertion or declaration of rights of way as a preliminary, for example, to inserting them on their own maps of local rights of way. Regrettably, however, such an administrative assertion would appear to have no legal consequences. It would not, for example, stop the running of negative prescription (discussed below) in relation to a little used public right of way.

Local authorities and public rights of way – Additional information

Section 46 of the 1967 Act imposes upon the relevant planning authorities a duty and not merely a power to assert public rights of way. To enable them to fulfil this duty the authorities are empowered, as the previous quotation indicates: 'to institute and defend legal proceedings and generally to take such steps they may deem expedient'. It is thought that they would be in breach of this duty if, having instituted such proceedings, they were to withdraw from them without due cause. There are statutory procedures enabling members of the public to take judicial and other steps to compel local authorities to fulfil their duties, but the subject is a large one outside the scope of this guide.[18]

This is the formal position in law, but in practice local authorities may well find it difficult to fulfil their duties under section 46. Frequently there are strongly opposed views on the part of those concerned and it may be difficult to ascertain the facts and to find evidence likely to be persuasive within a court of law. Litigation or prospective litigation involves extensive use of the authorities' relatively scarce resources and in consequence there may be a disposition to accept defeat or to seek a settlement acceptable to the parties concerned, but possibly unsatisfactory from the standpoint of the general public.

Creation of public rights of way

The creation of public rights of way depends largely upon the common law. This is the ancient customary or judge-made law of Scotland, as opposed to statute law. Under the common law, public rights of way may be created by usage. It has sometimes been asserted that public rights of way could be created by express grant but there has been some controversy about this. This is discussed in the additional information on page 102. A means to avoid that controversy may be for a landowner to acknowledge the existence of a public right of way by executing an appropriately worded deed. This would serve to bar the landowner personally from subsequently challenging the public right of way.

The more usual method by which public rights of way were established was by their continuous use by the public from time immemorial. Time immemorial came to mean forty years.[19] This period was reduced to a period of twenty years by the Prescription and Limitation (Scotland) Act 1973 ('the 1973 Act'), but otherwise that Act did little more than codify the common law in relation to rights of way.[20] A knowledge of that law, therefore, remains crucial. A knowledge of the relevant provision of the 1973 Act is also important.

In summary, the essential requirements for the creation of a public right of way under the common law are these:

> The route must run from one public place to a public place;
> The route must follow a more or less defined line;
> The route must have been used openly and peaceably by members of the public otherwise than with the permission, express or implied, of the landowner;
> It must have been so used without substantial and effective interruption for a period of 20 years or more.

Section 3(3) of the 1973 Act provides: 'If a public right of way over land has been possessed by the public for a continuous period of twenty years openly, peaceably, and without judicial interruption, then, as from the expiration of that period, the existence of the right of way as so possessed shall be exempt from challenge.'

These essential requirements will be considered briefly below. For ease of understanding, the third aspect in that list will be dealt with as two categories, namely 'used by members of the public in a manner not reliant on the landowner's permission' and 'openly and peaceably'.

A public right of way comes into existence or is 'constituted' from the moment when these essential requirements are met (subject to one specific qualification, where land has been acquired by a statutory undertaker such as a railway company, as discussed in the immediately following additional information).

There is no need for any formal legal or administrative procedure to constitute a right of way. A court decree of declarator (that is to say, a court ruling which declares something) does not create a public right of way, rather it merely confirms that such a right already exists (or does not exist). At present, the law provides no administrative process for confirming the existence of public rights of way.

Important statutory powers are conferred upon local authorities to assert, maintain, divert and even extinguish public rights of way. In addition, there are some statutory provisions that allow for access routes which are not expressed to be rights of way and are not catered for by access rights under the 2003 Act. Whatever the nature of the rights created, these powers primarily concern access authorities and supplement rather than alter the common law. For this reason they are considered separately and later in this guide.

Creation of public rights of way – Additional Information

In a recent property law textbook, Gretton and Steven note, 'In principle, a public right of way may be created expressly in a deed granted by the landowner.'[21] They then go on to explain how this might be done, however they do note that creation by deed is 'rare'.[22] That observation is consonant with the discussion in the case of *Hamilton* v *Dumfries and Galloway Council (No. 2)*,[23] although ScotWays is aware of a number of examples of deeds of acknowledgement and undertaking granted by landowners to such effect.

In one case parties wishing to make such a grant of access to the public purported to grant a deed conferring a 'servitude' right of access to members of the public.[24] This purported form of public servitude right appears to be a hybrid not recognised by Scots law. The multiplicity of potential holders of 'public' rights raises the question of whether a deed is appropriate (although a grant to a representative body or an access authority could avoid that criticism). Obscurity about whether such a deed requires subsequent possession to create the right is another consideration that fogs the issue somewhat. Meanwhile, although there are remarks by judges to the contrary, the prevailing judicial opinion is that the English doctrine of implied dedication of grant does not form part of the law of Scotland.[25]

It is noted above that where land is owned by a statutory undertaker such as a railway company this may prevent the public obtaining a public right of way over it. The case law is not satisfactory,[26] but this would perhaps be the case where the right is inconsistent with the purposes for which the undertaking was established and a particular parcel of land has been acquired for a specific purpose to do with that relevant undertaking. A convincing argument has been made to the contrary.[27] In relation specifically to railways, in 2013 the matter of railway level crossings was considered across Great Britain by the law reform bodies of Scotland and England and Wales, in a way that suggests rights can currently be acquired by prescription over land owned by statutory undertakings, but also in a way that could put the matter beyond doubt in that context. The Law Commission and Scottish Law Commission Report on Level Crossings recommends that there should be 'statutory provision to the effect that no public right of way across any part of the railway track may be acquired by prescription.'[28] The Report has not been implemented.

In theory, a right of way could cross (for example) a railway where it existed before the railway was built. However, in practice, pre-existing rights are usually extinguished by the legislation relating to the statutory undertaker.[29]

This guide will now consider the aspects of the prescriptive process whereby a right of way is created. Please note this is a technical area of law and reference should be made to specialist texts for relevant guidance, including Johnston, *Prescription and Limitation*,[30] and Cusine and Paisley, *Servitudes and Rights of Way*.[31] Aspects 3, 4 and 5 for creation of rights of way (set out below) are highlighted in section 3(3) of the 1973 Act, which requires that a public right of way is 'possessed by the public for a continuous period of twenty years openly, peaceably, and without judicial interruption' before it can be created through positive prescription. Section 3(3) makes no reference to the need for public termini or the need to follow a more or less defined line, meaning reference must be made to the common law for those aspects.

On the creation of a public right of passage for the purposes of the Roads (Scotland) Act 1984, reference can be made to *Scottish Roads Law*.[32] One of the means is establishment of a public right of way.

Creation of public rights of way: (1) public place to public place

Towards the beginning of this chapter, a brief definition of a public right of way was set out. As explained there, and developed in more detail here, it is a right of passage from 'a place where the public are entitled to be to a place where the public are entitled to be, as from one part of a public road to another part of a public road, or from one village to another village, and so forth.'[33]

Rights of way are accordingly predicated on having public termini: if either end is not a public place, there will be no right of way. The definition given above hints that public roads and villages can be public. In *Marquis of Bute* v *McKirdy* Lord Moncrieff said: 'A public place is one to which the public have right of access, which the public have right to occupy, and which in fact the public do occupy by a practice of resort.[34] Clear examples of public places would include a village or town, a church[35] or public burial ground, a ferry or harbour and a public road or highway.

A private road may also for this purpose be a public place if it is proved that the public have unrestricted access to it.[36] It has been suggested that a circular route can constitute a public right of way,[37] as may a cul-de-sac.[38] Any point on a public right of way will itself be a public place. It has also been held that where members of the public used a man-made walkway to get from one part of the town to another to use banks, the swimming pool, a church, leisure facilities, schools etc. that was sufficient to constitute the walkway a public right of way.[39] However, it is not enough to demonstrate that the public go to a place to constitute it a public place, because the public may be excluded from some 'public' places, from time to time. Thus, it seems that railway stations,[40] bus stations, airports[41] and most reservoirs are not public places for the purposes of public rights of way. This will also exclude some markets.

Under Scots law, the foreshore normally belongs to the Crown and the public generally have a right to walk along it. That is not necessarily enough to make it a public place for the purposes of establishing a public right of way. The public should be in the habit of resorting to it for loading or unloading vessels, for fishing, or for some other definite purpose.[42] The regular use of the foreshore by members of the public for purposes of recreation may be a sufficiently definite purpose in this context. (General access rights to the foreshore are discussed below.)

It has been judicially stated that, where there is sufficient evidence of resort to the particular spot, the bank of a navigable river may be a public place at which a public right of way may end.[43]

Creation of public rights of way: (1) public place to public place –
Additional Information

In *PIK Facilities Ltd* v *Watson's Ayr Park Ltd*,[44] Prestwick Airport was held not to be a public place, on the basis that the public does not have a right to access it at all times. Similarly, a sub-post office within a private home[45] has also been refused public place status, as was a cattle market open for only four days a week,[46] although markets that have only been open twice a year have been taken to be public places.[47]

For two centuries or more the public, often in large numbers, have been resorting to the tops of the Scottish hills for recreational purposes. It seems doubtful, however, whether under the present law those tops would be regarded as 'public places' or places where 'the public are entitled to be' in relation to the constitution of a public right of way.[48] Although a top might be accessible through exercise of the new access rights, it must be remembered that these rights may be superseded by statute; this possibility is unhelpful to the argument that a top might be a 'public place'.

Creation of public rights of way: (2) a more or less defined route

It is also a general requirement for establishing a public right of way in Scotland that the public use should follow a more or less defined route. Ongoing yet aimless perambulation will not create a right of way, but at the other end of the spectrum it is not necessary to prove that the public have followed a definite path or track. Where a decision has been given for the pursuer in an action of declarator of public right of way, the court has power to fix its precise line, if necessary, by remitting the question to a surveyor.

Minor deviations are of no importance either in the context of the creation of a public right of way or in that of its subsequent use. The extent of deviation permissible will depend upon the nature of the countryside: what is permissible in wilder areas might be impermissible elsewhere. Deviations may be necessitated, for example, by a change in the course of a river where the public right of way follows the bank, or by a landslip where the route is along a cliff edge, and wet weather may make a detour necessary to avoid swampy ground, but the route must in principle be capable of use from end to end. For the creation of a public right of way it is helpful, but not indispensable, to establish that the route followed by the public right of way is the most direct one available.

In relation to water, there is a long established public right of navigation in the tidal parts of rivers, and it is unnecessary that the navigation should be from one public place to another. In relation to non-tidal parts of rivers, the House of Lords has held that rights of navigation over such parts are not to be assimilated to public rights of way over land. While their existence must be established by habitual use from 'time immemorial', traditionally forty years, the route need not be between two public places and the rights are not lost by non-use.[49] The position in relation to lochs remains to be clarified. However, the 2003 Act gives statutory rights of access to all inland water, for non-motorised use (see above, page 44).

Creation of public rights of way: (2) a more or less defined route –
Additional Information

It has been said that 'the privilege of wandering upon the face of an unenclosed hill, though it be for half a century, will not confer a right of way.'[50] That said, it is not necessary to prove that the public have followed a definite path or track as opposed to a more or less consistent and generally defined line. It has been explained: 'In many instances in Scotland, where there are moors to be passed over, the public have right of way, and yet they may have used twenty different lines for going from one terminus to the other, taking the one they liked best or found most suitable, in the state of the ground and of the weather.'[51]

In relation to the need (or otherwise) for a direct route, in *Rhins District Committee* v *Cuninghame*, Lord Sands remarked: 'A person may have reasons of his own for preferring a roundabout road, or even business on the way constrains him to do so. Nor does it matter, I think, that the gaining of the other terminus is not the main or an important object of the journey. It suffices that it obviates the necessity of returning by the way one came, and affords a pleasant round.'[52]

It will be observed that section 3(3) of the 1973 Act refers to a public right of way over land and so does not regulate the position relating to rights of way or passage of vessels over rivers and lochs. (Unlike the 2003 Act, the 1973 Act does not expressly define land as including inland waters.)

Creation of public rights of way: (3) use by the public as of right

Section 3(3) of the 1973 Act states that a public right of way can be constituted only by members of the public 'possessing' the route, in the sense of actually passing over the whole route with a fair degree of regularity. This reflects the common law and the possession must be of the whole route.[53] The amount of use is a question of the circumstances of each individual case. In a thinly populated area less use would be required than in a densely populated district. This has been explained as follows: 'The question is ... whether, having regard to the sparseness or density of the population, the [use] over the prescriptive period was in degree and quality such as might have been expected if the road had been an undisputed right of way.'[54] Accordingly, the fact that there was little or no evidence of a route's use during the winter months did not prevent the Court holding that there was a public right of way from Clova to Braemar via Glen Doll (Jock's Road).[55]

It is sometimes said that the public use must be as a matter of right or of supposed right. This means the use must not be referable to the express grant of the landowner or tolerance or acquiescence on his part. A proprietor would be regarded as tolerating the use of a route by his tenants or employees, or even by persons who visit him for professional or business purposes. Where a landowner expressly constitutes a servitude right of way in favour of the owners of adjacent land, the use of it by those persons and members of their households and employees is regarded as deriving from the express grant of the servitude right rather than from the possible existence of a public right of way. It is otherwise where the servitude right extends only to a part of the route. In that case the use by those persons of the whole route would not be disregarded in determining whether there is a public right of way over the whole route.[56]

Creation of public rights of way: (3) use by the public as of right –
Additional information

Cases such as *Jenkins* v *Murray*,[57] *Mackintosh* v *Moir*,[58] *Magistrates of Edinburgh* v *North British Railway Co.*,[59] and *Norrie* v *Magistrates of Kirriemuir*[60] provide authority that possession must be as of right. The concept of 'use as of right' is an elusive one, but is possibly best understood as being use of a type and character consistent only with the uncontested exercise of a public right of way rather than use referable to the express grant of the owner of the land or mere tolerance or acquiescence on his part.[61] There may be situations where the requisite possession for the establishing of a public right of way commenced by virtue of tolerance or acquiescence on the part of the proprietor but evolves into an assertion of a right.[62]

It was noted above that section 5(5) of the 2003 Act provides that the exercise of access rights does not of itself amount to possession for the purposes of positively prescribing a right of way. This will, in many circumstances, rule out access taken by foot or on a bicycle or horseback from any calculation. This does not mean that arguments about the constitution or rights of way by prescription will no longer happen. For example, *PIK Facilities Ltd* v *Watson's Ayr Park Ltd*[63] was about vehicular access. Such cases are not affected by the 2003 Act. Of more relevance to this guide would be access that has been taken over ground that has been excluded under section 6 of the 2003 Act. Any such access would not be 'exercise of access rights' and could therefore be included in any prescriptive reckoning as to whether and for how long access has been taken. Given the nature of the exclusions in section 6 (and the likely vigilance of landowners in these areas), such instances are likely to be rare.

A question arises as to whether an obstruction which is easily surmounted has the effect of interrupting the period of prescriptive use required to constitute a public right of way. As to this, Lord McLaren has said: 'But, of course, the mere putting up of a gate would not run against the acquisition of the road by the public if it was left open, if it formed no substantial impediment to the use of the road by the public and if, in point of fact, the public continued to use the road as it was used before.'[64]

Any suggestion that the use required to establish the existence of a public right of way must have been for business or commercial purposes appears to be erroneous. It seems clear that recreational use alone may be sufficient to establish the existence of a public right of way, although recreational use will now often be ascribable to the 2003 Act.

Creation of public rights of way: (4) 'openly, peaceably'

It is a requirement of the common law that the use must not have been by stealth or violence but open and peaceful, of such a quality as to indicate clearly to the proprietor that a right of passage is being asserted. If in these circumstances the proprietor intervenes with some resolution and consistency to stop persons using the route, their possession or use is not peaceable.[65] If the proprietor does not so intervene, it is assumed that he acquiesces in the use of the claimed public right of way.

Creation of public rights of way: (4) 'openly, peaceably' –
Additional information

It has been observed that the amount and quantity of use alone might be relied upon to exclude any argument by the landowner that the use is a mere tolerance and also that there is no need to demonstrate any conflict between the use made by the public and that of the landowner to establish a right of way.[66]

It has been judicially stated in the context of the general law of prescription, that the claimant cannot rely on acts of possession (i.e. use), 'unless he is able to show that they were either known, or ought to have been known to [the] owner or to persons to whom he entrusted the charge of his property.'[67] This rule may seem harsh, but the courts tend to assume that a landowner, personally or through his staff, will be vigilant to assert his rights.[68] Where it is shown, in a sparsely populated rural area, that there has been as much use as could be expected for that kind of area, without any attempt to hide it from the landowner, the applicability of this line of thinking might be questioned.

Creation of public rights of way: (5) 'For a continuous period of twenty years . . . without judicial interruption'

Apart from shortening the period of presumptive use from 40 years to 20, the 1973 Act did not make any other significant reforms: the law for the creation of public rights of way was otherwise restated.

The 'continuous period' of which the common law required proof did not necessarily have to be the period of forty years ending at the date specified by the pursuer, still less the period of forty years ending at the date of the action.[69]

Similar principles, it is thought, apply under the 1973 Act. Section 3(3) of the 1973 Act also asks for a 'continuous period'. The use of the term 'continuous' does not imply that the route must have been used constantly, but only so often as is consistent with public use as of right, having regard to the nature of the route and the density of the population.[70] The use of the term also indicates that there must have been no substantial and effective interruption to the public's use of the route during the prescriptive period. Thus the restriction of public access to four days a week would prevent the establishment of the existence of a public right of way.[71] A brief interruption is not fatal, but any action by the proprietor which effectively closes the route for a period and which is acquiesced in by its users, will interrupt the prescription. For example, Waverley Station in Edinburgh closes each day in the early hours of the morning, which would prevent a public right of way being constituted. It is sometimes thought that it is sufficient for a proprietor to close the route for a day, or for a few days, each year, but if there is evidence of continuous use, such action may be ineffective unless the proprietor can show that the closure of the route was acquiesced in by its ordinary users.[72]

'Judicial interruption' is an entirely different matter. Under the general law of prescription in Scotland the required continuity of possession is deemed to be interrupted by the commencement of proceedings designed to challenge the alleged right. This has nothing to do with the practical interruption of the exercise of the alleged right. The commencement of the proceedings unequivocally demonstrates lack of acquiescence on the part of the proprietor.

Creation of public rights of way: (5) 'For a continuous period of twenty years . . . without judicial interruption' – Additional information

Section 14(1)(a) of the 1973 Act permits that prescriptive period of twenty years to apply retrospectively, i.e. before the Act came into force on 25 July 1976. That being the case, on general principles of statutory interpretation, this new regime should not exclude proof that a public right of way existed at a date prior to the coming into force of the Act. This is now largely academic: if there is no evidence of any use of a route since 1976 any right of way would probably have fallen out of use. That said, in the relatively recent case of *North East Fife DC* v *Nisbet*[73] usage from the 1920s was crucial in establishing a right of way which had not been lost thereafter. (Extinction is discussed below.)

Where the route of an old public right of way has been shifted for the common convenience of the proprietor and the users of the public right of way, the period of use of the earlier route may be accumulated with that of the later route in calculating the total period of continuous use.

Successful creation of a right of way: exemption from challenge, 'as so possessed'

Once a public right of way has been created by twenty years' use, the public's right to use the route is exempt from challenge. This means it will subsist unless and until the conditions required for the extinction of the right are fulfilled (discussed below, this being something an interested landowner would need to prove on the balance of probabilities).

In terms of the nature of the right that is exempt from challenge, the words 'as so possessed' are of some significance. They reflect the common law rule that 'possession' (or use) by persons on foot would not create a right in favour of persons on horseback, or use by persons on horseback rights in relation to the droving of cattle or use by vehicular traffic. Despite that apparent scepticism of allowing less onerous use to blossom into access by other means, case law has allowed for some adaptation to reflect new technology. Thus, on the introduction of wheeled carts into agricultural Scotland, it was held that a route hitherto used only for the passage of cattle, or by persons on horseback or on foot, might also 'be used by carts if the route was capable, without further works, of being traversed by carts from one end to the other'.[74] A similar decision was subsequently given relating to the use by motor vehicles of a road previously used by carts and horse drawn carriages.[75]

In Scotland, in relation to public rights of way created by prescription, the greater right includes the lesser, so that a person can walk over a public right of way for carriages or motor vehicles.

Successful creation of a right of way: exemption from challenge, 'as so possessed' – Additional information

The words 'exempt from challenge' must be read subject to section 8 of the 1973 Act, which relates, amongst other things, to the extinction of public rights of way.

The words 'as so possessed' may also imply that it is the established route and not any later variation from it that is free from future challenge. This, however, does not exclude the subsequent variation of the public right of way by agreement, by acquiescence or by judicial or statutory determination.

The manner of the exercise of a right of way

Any passage via a public right of way should be conducted in a way that minimises the impact on the interests of the landowner. This can be thought of as analogous to the rule that applies in relation to private servitudes, that the dominant proprietor must exercise rights in a manner that is *civiliter*, with as little disturbance to the landowner as possible. Regard must also be had to the rights of others using the land, albeit there is no statutory exhortation to use a right of way responsibly that compares to the 2003 Act. This does not mean users of a right of way can behave with impunity. Naturally, criminal law will continue to apply, including some criminal offences that are of particular relevance. Pertinent examples include the rules about obstructing someone else using a right of way (under section 53 of the Civic Government (Scotland) Act 1982) or regulating fires next to a right of way (under section 3 of the Trespass (Scotland) Act 1865 (as amended by the 2003 Act, which allows fires lit in a responsible access context) and section 56 of the Civic Government (Scotland) Act 1982). Reference can be made to the relevant offences digested in the Access Code, Appendix 1. Further, the civil law of nuisance (which is normally relevant to objectionable use of land by the owner) could apply to restrict obnoxious behaviour by a user of a right of way.

Duties of the landowner in relation to rights of way

The most important duty incumbent on the owner of land traversed by a right of way is a passive one. She must allow appropriate passage without interference. In the event of interference, a court order can be obtained to regulate future conduct, and any breach of a relevant order can be penalised by the court (including with a fine).

Specific criminal offences exist to criminalise actions that undermine or obstruct a right of way. One of those is found in the 2003 Act, with section 23 criminalising the non-reinstatement of a right of way (and a core path) after ploughing or otherwise disturbing a route. Interference with a road (which by statute includes a public right of way, as explained below) can also be a criminal offence, as detailed below.

Positive duties play much less of a role in relation to rights of way. As noted in chapter 2, a landowner must conduct herself in a manner that is responsible in relation to land where access rights under the 2003 Act are exercisable. There is not the same general positive duty in relation to rights of way.

The older authorities suggested that under the common law the proprietor or occupier of the land owed no positive duties to persons using a public right of way and that, even when the route presented a danger to the public, she need not repair the route (although she would need to suffer its repair by others to allow for the appropriate level of use to take place again, discussed below on page 120). As to whether a landowner would need to give notice of any danger, this seems unlikely when a danger is obvious.[76] This question would be covered by the general rules of occupiers' liability (discussed below, in chapter 4).

Under the common law the owner of the ground is entitled to erect gates and stiles so long as they do not materially obstruct the use of the route of a public right of way.[77] The onus is on the landowner to show that no material obstruction is caused.[78] In relation to land which is being used for agriculture or forestry the common law is supplemented by a statutory provision allowing the erection of stiles and gates, but the landowner must seek the permission of the local planning authority.[79] This mixed provision of common law and statute is now augmented by the more comprehensive provisions relative to obstructions in the 2003 Act which apply equally to public rights of way and the statutory access rights.

Section 14 of the 2003 Act means the owner of land traversed by a public right of way is prohibited from acting (or omitting to act) in a way that hinders or disincentives access, unless the landowner's choices can be ascribed to proper land management. Anything that contravenes section 14 can be followed with enforcement action by the relevant access authority. These rules are discussed above on page 68.

The fact that a public right of way falls within roads legislation brings a number of consequences: for example, a person commits an offence if in or under a road she executes works or makes excavations which constitute a danger or which she permits to become a danger.[80] Further implications are considered below.

Duties of the landowner in relation to rights of way – Additional information

> *Fife Council* v *Nisbet*[81] provides an example of landowner interference. As noted in chapter 1 of this guide, the relevant route was declared to be a right of way in a court action in 1997. An interdict was imposed at that time requiring the landowners not to obstruct the right of way or interfere with its use. When interference took place, each of them was fined £500.

Obstructions

A mixture of common law and statutory rules now governs the obstruction of public rights of way. Some of these rules also apply to access rights in general or core paths in particular under the 2003 Act, which will be highlighted where relevant.

The common law does not permit a public right of way to be obstructed to any material extent and any form of obstruction to a public right of way must be justified by the proprietor as non-material.[82] He is not entitled permanently to restrict the width of a public right of way, even where the reduced width is sufficient to allow pedestrian passage.[83] However, the proprietor can restrict the width for a short period whilst he carries out necessary works on an adjacent building or land. Such an obstruction may be non-material if it lasts for a short period, but it could be material if it is intended to be a permanent obstruction. The length of time an obstruction endures is a factor in determining whether it is material.

The proprietor is not entitled to lock or indeed to wire up a gate in a manner that cannot be removed by a member of the public, for however short a period, nor may he erect a fence or wall across a pedestrian right of way without providing a gate or stile. Where a proprietor does so, the remedy of a person obstructed, in principle at least, is to remove as much of any 'recent' obstruction as is necessary in order to restore free passage to the public.[84] A person doing this does take something of a risk, because it will not always be clear whether an obstruction is 'recent' or, indeed, whether the route is in fact a public right of way. Where the matter is doubtful the walker acts at his peril and may be liable in damages to the proprietor if it eventually turns out that the route is not a public right of way. He may also be charged with breaches of the criminal law, including the offence of 'malicious mischief'. A further consideration is that a decision not to act against the obstruction could contribute to the interruption then eventual loss of the right of way by the process of negative prescription. This is discussed in additional information.

As mentioned above, a proprietor is entitled to erect stiles on a public right of way for pedestrians and, if they are reasonably necessary, gates on a public right of way for carriages or cattle. The gates, however, must be such that they can be opened and shut without undue difficulty and, even if openable must not give the appearance of being unopenable. Users of public rights of way should always see that gates are left as they are found, not only as a matter of courtesy but also because they have a duty so to do under the law of nuisance. Advice about gates is provided under the Access Code (at paragraphs 4.7–4.9 and Part 5, page 95).

The application of the Roads (Scotland) Act 1984 to public rights of way means section 59 (control of obstructions on roads) applies to them. It is an offence to create an obstruction on a public right of way without the roads authority's consent in writing. Any person who creates such an obstruction may be obliged to remove it when required by the roads authority or a constable in uniform. The roads authority has power to remove such obstructions and to reinstate the route.[85] It also has power to require the removal of obstructing trees and shrubs.[86]

Where the local authority is of the opinion that a barbed wire fence or electrified fence is likely to be injurious to a person lawfully using the route, it may require the occupier of the land to take specified steps to remove the danger.[87]

It will be recalled that where access rights apply under the 2003 Act, the Access Code provides that land managers must not obstruct any path or track without reasonable cause, in terms of section 14.

The main statutory provision relating to the obstruction of public rights of way, section 46(1) of the 1967 Act, has been set out in full on page 99 above. The planning authorities have a duty to 'keep clear and free from obstruction or encroachment any public right of way which is wholly or partly within their area'. Ploughing may form an obstruction and, in this guide, this is dealt with in the context of the statutory access rights (with reference to section 23 of the 2003 Act) (see page 67).

Misleading notices and animals are discussed below.

Obstructions – Additional information

A walker who encounters an obstruction is faced with a species of devil's alternative. If there is a public right of way and he fails to remove or to bypass the obstruction, the use of the public right of way may be regarded as having been interrupted. On the other hand, if it turns out that there is no public right of way, the walker commits an unlawful act if he removes the obstruction. In the past the attitude of procurators fiscal was not to intervene, on the ground that the matter was essentially a civil one, but the Court has recently been less inclined to condone persons taking the law into their own hands.

In the case of *Clark* v *Syme*,[88] the Lord Justice General remarked that 'The mere fact that his criminal act was performed under a misconception of what legal remedies he might otherwise have does not make it any the less criminal.' Lord Carmont in the same case said that: 'If the respondent found the situation intolerable, the proper thing to do was to invoke the assistance of the civil courts in the ordinary way.'

Obstructions can have a role in terms of interrupting the period of prescriptive use required to constitute a public right of way, as discussed above. Interruption that takes place before any right of way is constituted will, naturally, be less susceptible to regulation.

Notices

A common form of disincentive is the misleading notice. Examples could be:

'*Private*' (the notice may stand on private[ly owned] ground, but there may be a public right of way over it);

'*Private road*' (the road may be a private one in relation to vehicles or in terms of roads legislation, and yet open to pedestrians);

'*Trespassers will be prosecuted*' (in general, private rights of prosecution for trespass are not available in Scotland, plus the simple act of non-harmful trespass will not always be a crime).

In the context of public rights of way, such notices are misleading and are best ignored. It is not suggested that members of the public should themselves remove such notices since, in a literal sense, they do not obstruct free passage. It is possible, however, that members of the public affected may have other remedies open to them, including actions of interdict and even, where they have suffered loss or injury, e.g. as a result of their having to take a detour, an action of damages. Individuals should also consider notifying the relevant access authority, as the 2003 Act prohibits landowners from deterring those using rights of way or access rights by erecting notices.

Signage about risks relating to the characteristics of the land might encourage members of the public to exercise caution. These are not objectionable where they are appropriate, and indeed appropriate signage can play a role in determining occupiers' liability. Occupiers' liability is discussed in chapter 4.

Signs about animals deserve some consideration, in the context of dissuading access with an animal and in the context of using or simply mentioning animals to discourage access unjustifiably.

A permanent sign declaring 'no dogs allowed' is difficult to justify, as a walker is generally entitled to be accompanied by her dog provided the dog is under control. (This will particularly be the case where a dog provides necessary assistance to its keeper.) That said, there will be specific circumstances or contexts where a sign regulating access with dogs could be justified, such as certain areas of formal gardens and where the unexpected presence of dogs would be problematic for legitimate land management. Someone staying on a public right of way with a dog is unlikely to face such challenges, although it will be recalled some criminal offences relating to dogs could apply (relating to dog fouling and livestock worrying).

Turning to the other issue, a potentially misleading notice is a sign saying 'Beware of the bull' or similar. The implications of a bull actually being present will be considered below, but for now it can be noted that if signage is genuinely needed, clear pictures and/or wording should be used and any supplementary wording considered carefully. Signs about guard dogs can – indeed, must – be displayed for areas where there are guard dogs.[89] It is possible for enclosures with guard dogs to be adjacent to rights of way, but there are rules that guard dogs must have a handler present or be suitably secured in the premises, so this should not be overly problematic for those using a right of way.

Notices – Additional information

To offer some more thoughts on signage, a sign that proclaims 'Private' could be argued to be accurate in the sense that it is declaring it is not 'public' (i.e. owned via a public body or indeed by a charity that welcomes the public to its land). With the preponderance of private landowners in Scotland, it can be questioned how necessary such signage is. Under section 151 of the 1984 Act, a 'private road' merely means a road which the roads authority has no duty to maintain. Such a road may be a public right of way and accordingly signs proclaiming '*private road*' do not necessarily mean there is no right of access.

Regarding bulls, the suggestions about signage come from the Health and Safety Executive. Its role is considered further below, but for now it is worth bearing in mind its general advice (delivered by way of an information sheet).[90] After issuing a reminder that 'you should have made every effort not to keep aggressive, or potentially aggressive, animals in a field or area where the public commonly take access', the HSE information sheet notes 'it is good practice to display signs informing the public when a bull or cows with calves are in the area.' Signs should be put at strategic locations and it is stated that 'Supplementary text should not suggest that the bull is aggressive, threatening or dangerous (i.e. avoid words such as "beware" or "danger").'

Animals

The keeper of a bull or other animal with dangerous propensities may be interdicted from allowing it to graze on unfenced land adjoining a public right of way.[91] Under statute law it is an offence for any person to suffer or permit any creature in his charge to cause danger or injury to any other person who is in a public place or to give such person reasonable cause for alarm.[92]

In relation specifically to bulls and public rights of way, the occupier of a field or enclosure through which there is a public right of way commits an offence under the 1967 Act if he permits any bull to be at large within it, unless the bull is not more than ten months old or is not of one of the recognised dairy breeds and is at large in any field with cows or heifers.[93] These exceptions, however, would not necessarily help a person prosecuted under other provisions. For example, under Health and Safety at Work legislation it is the duty both of employers and of self-employed persons to conduct their undertakings so as to ensure, so far as reasonably practicable, that third parties who may be affected are not exposed to risks to their health and safety and that breach of this duty is an offence.[94] The Health and Safety Executive has a role in relation to this and has issued guidance through an information sheet for farmers, landowners and other livestock keepers.[95] It makes a number of suggestions, and states that you cannot use the presence of an animal, e.g. a bull, to deter walkers from accessing a core path or public footpath.

Maintenance of, and prevention of damage to, rights of way

At common law the proprietor of ground traversed by a public right of way is under no obligation to maintain or repair the route or bridges on the route.[96] This would appear to be the position even when a route presents a danger to the public,[97] although there is the possibility of civil liability arising under the rules surrounding occupiers' liability (discussed in chapter 4). The proprietor may, if he wishes, fence off the route of the public right of way from his other ground, provided that he leaves sufficient space for whatever type of traffic is entitled to use it.

The public may repair the track of a public right of way and, in accordance with the general law relating to servitudes, the proprietor should allow the public reasonable access for the purpose of maintaining the route.[98] But they may not, in doing this, encroach upon or damage the owner's property.[99] The public's right would extend to such operations as cutting back bushes, improving marshy places, bridging streams, erecting stiles and, generally, to any operations which would improve the public right of way without injuriously affecting the proprietor's interest.[100] A view has been expressed that such operations might well include the provision of seats but the legal authority for this point is slight.[101]

These common law rules have now been supplemented by statute, giving an important role to local government. The much wider role of access authorities with regard to statutory access rights has already been noted. In relation to rights of way, as we have seen, the planning authority has a duty to 'keep open and free from obstruction or encroachment any public right of way' wholly or partly within their area. A planning authority has a power to 'repair and maintain any public right of way (not being a road or footway at the side of a road) within their area'.[102] This power, however, does not relieve any other authority or person on whom primary liability in respect of such repair or maintenance may fall. If, moreover, a public right of way is properly classified as a 'private road' under the Roads (Scotland) Act 1984, a local roads authority has power to contribute to or carry out maintenance work on them.[103]

Under section 54 of the 1967 Act, a planning authority may, in relation to public rights of way which are wholly or partly within its area (and any relevant public paths or long-distance routes) make byelaws for the preservation of order, for the prevention of damage, and for avoiding interference with the enjoyment of the land by others. Such byelaws are not allowed to interfere with the exercise of any public right of way or navigation, in terms of section 54(6).

Signposting

ScotWays has erected several thousand signposts throughout Scotland. Its practice is always to seek the consent of the proprietors concerned. By statute, planning authorities may erect and maintain signposts and direction posts on public rights of way, and other persons may do so on public rights of way which are not public roads with the consent of the planning authority.[104] The proprietor of the land may erect direction signs to indicate the route provided, of course, they are not misleading or of such a large scale as to block the route.

Diversion of public rights of way

Public rights of way, unlike rights of access under the 2003 Act, are only exercisable over a fixed route. At common law a proprietor is not entitled to substitute an alternative route for the route of an existing public right of way. No doubt in practice such alternative routes have been accepted by the public, e.g. where a public right of way has been diverted from an original line running too close to, or through, the grounds of a private house.

Statutory provision allows the owner, tenant or occupier of land crossed by a footpath or bridleway that is a public right of way to apply to the planning authority for a diversion order in relation to it. Section 35 of the 1967 Act, alongside schedule 3, applies in relation to the appropriate diversion of footpaths and bridleways that are rights of way; it continues to apply in this context despite the repeal of many provisions of Part 3 of the 1967 Act in other contexts.[105] Such a diversion will only be authorised where it is expedient for the efficient use of the land (or of other land held therewith) or providing a shorter or more convenient path across the land. Further, the diversion should not be substantially less convenient to the public and an order for diversion can only confirmed after having regard to the effect the diversion would have on: public enjoyment of the path as a whole; other land served by the right of way; and land over which the right of way is to be created and any land held therewith.

There is also provision in sections 202 and 207 of the 1997 Act for the stopping up or diversion of roads by order where that is necessary in the context of development, to enable such approved development to take place. Similar provision is made in section 208 of the 1997 Act for the stopping up or diversion of any footpath or bridleway where that is necessary in the context of approved development, with scope for the planning authority to create an alternative route or improve an existing route to replace the stopped up or diverted route, or to carry out works in relation to a diverted, created or improved route. Section 208 of the 1997 Act also applies to core paths within the meaning of the 2003 Act, as detailed in chapter 2.

Extinction and suspension of public rights of way: the common law

There are important statutory powers relating to the extinguishing of public rights of way, as explained below, but the starting position of the common law rule is still important.

Under the common law a public right of way was extinguished where it was proved that the public had failed to exercise or enforce it from time immemorial, fixed by judicial construction at forty years. This was changed to a period of twenty years by the Prescription and Limitation (Scotland) Act 1973. Section 8 of that Act declares that if 'the right has subsisted for a continuous period of twenty years unexercised or unenforced, and without any relevant claim in relation to it having been made, then as from the expiration of that period the right shall be extinguished'. This process is called negative prescription.

The rule in section 8, with its relatively short prescriptive period of twenty years, makes it vitally important for users of public rights of way to exercise their rights of passage, particularly upon less frequently-used routes, and to do so resolutely if necessary. It is true that less evidence is required to keep an existing public right of way than to establish a new one but, if the public do not exercise their rights of passage, there is a risk that even historically important routes, such as parts of the roads built by General Wade or by Major William Caulfeild, will cease to be public rights of way. It is worth remembering that the failure of a roads authority to maintain a road does not necessarily mean that it loses its public character.[106] The non-use of a public right of way for carriages, carts and cattle would not necessarily imply its extinction as a public right of way for travellers on foot.[107] Section 8 refers only to a public right of way over land. A right of passage on a river or a natural loch is not subject to loss by disuse.[108]

Extinction and suspension of public rights of way: the common law – Additional information

> The common law rule requiring forty years of non-use would still apply in the unlikely event of a claim that a public right of way was extinguished as at a date prior to 25 July 1976. For extinction on or after 26 July 1976, the twenty-year period applies (that is to say, the twenty year rule does not only apply to extinctions commencing after it came into force, but also in respect of a period commencing on or after 26 July 1956).[109]

Extinction and suspension of public rights of way: powers of planning and other authorities

A public right of way is not necessarily extinguished when a public road has been laid down on the line of a public right of way. The matter is of little importance until the road falls into disuse. If no 'stopping up order' is made, the public right of way continues.[110] A stopping up order in relation to vehicular traffic will not necessarily extinguish a public right of way for pedestrians.[111] Even if the order relates to pedestrian use, a new public right of way may subsequently be created by use over the prescriptive period (this being acknowledged in the case of *Hamilton* v *Dumfries and Galloway Council (No. 2)*,[112] albeit that particular stopped up road had not been suitably used for prescriptive purposes). The position is much the same where a road has been realigned. The effective closure of the old route to vehicles and stock will not of itself cause it to cease to be a right of way for pedestrians.

Stopping up orders are made under the Roads (Scotland) Act 1984 and relative regulations, ordinarily on the basis that the road has become dangerous or is unnecessary. Such an order may provide for the stopping up of the road subject to the reservation of means of passage for pedestrians, cyclists, or both: in two special cases, the closure of a road must not be such as to obstruct a public right of way.[113] There are also some relevant powers in the Town and Country Planning (Scotland) Act 1997. It is possible to object to proposed stopping up orders, in which case an order must be confirmed by the Scottish Ministers before it has effect. One recent example where that confirmation was not provided related to a right of way in Culross, Fife, as explained in additional information.

By statute, certain public bodies may acquire land free of rights of way or may subsequently be empowered to take steps to secure their suspension or extinction. Public rights of way are occasionally closed to permit open cast coal extraction,[114] and for a variety of other purposes.[115] The status of public rights of way is not generally affected by land designations, for example as a country park,[116] a nature reserve,[117] or a site of special scientific interest.[118] The users of rights of way within these places, however, may be subject to byelaws regulating their use, and this will certainly be so in the case of nature reserves and sites of special scientific interest, although these byelaws must not interfere with the exercise of public rights of way.

Extinction and suspension of public rights of way: powers of planning and other authorities – Additional information

Stopping up powers are contained in sections 12, 68, 69, 70 and 152(2) of the 1984 Act and also in sections 202, 207 and 208 of the 1997 Act. The latter three provisions are discussed above in the context of diversions. The provisions under the 1984 Act are context specific and lay down how such stopping up orders are to be made in such specific circumstances: for example, an order under section 68 can be made when a road has become dangerous or is (or will become) unnecessary, but the roads authority must satisfy themselves that a suitable alternative road exists or that no alternative road is necessary before making an order. For further information on stopping up in the context of roads, reference should be made to the statute itself and *Scottish Roads Law*.[119] It must be remembered that using any of these powers to change a right of way will not change any core path that exists along the same alignment. Separate powers exist for changing the alignment of core paths.

Section 206 of the 1997 Act can also play a role in relation to land which has been acquired or appropriated for planning purposes. It empowers the Scottish Ministers by order to extinguish any public right of way over land where they are satisfied that there is an alternative route or that such a route is not required. Section 203 of the 1997 Act confers a similar power upon planning authorities for the conversion of highways over which the public has a right of way for vehicles into footpaths or bridleways and for the stopping up or diversion of footpaths or bridleways.

The example of a successful objection highlighted above related to a route of approximately 47 metres between the streets of Mid Causeway and Low Causeway, Culross. This had been used for more than 30 years as a short cut between the two streets. The objectors (who were represented by Culross Community Council) argued for the retention of the right of way that Fife Council wished to stop up to enable development (in terms of section 208 of the 1997 Act). The objections triggered paragraph 5 of Schedule 16, meaning the order needed approval from the Scottish Ministers before it would have effect. The reporter appointed by the Scottish Ministers to consider the matter found the route provided an important relief from the adverse circumstances of historic cobbled streets in Culross (particularly for those using wheelchairs or pushing prams) and also noted its retention would prevent an additional safety risk that steering users to other (busier) routes would cause. Accordingly, the public benefit of retaining the right of way outweighed any advantage which would arise from the implementation of the planning permission.[120]

Reference can also be made to section 34 of the 1967 Act which, like section 35, also survives in relation to rights of way notwithstanding the repeal of Part 3 of the 1967 in many other circumstances. It allows for the closure of public paths (meaning footpaths and bridleways) where they are not needed for public use, subject to the procedure laid down in that section and Schedule 3 of the 1967 Act.

Court actions relating to public rights of way

As explained on page 99 above, planning authorities have a duty to assert and protect public rights of way and to this end may institute and defend legal proceedings[121] and intervene in actions[122] by others relating to public rights of way. However, any member of the public who can show an interest may bring an action to establish the existence of a public right of way or to defend proceedings designed to deny the existence of such a right. The interest need not be substantial. While, generally speaking, any resident in the neighbourhood would be assumed to have an interest, it is not necessary for the person bringing the action to reside locally. A person who is in the habit of walking in the district may raise or defend proceedings, though he may reside at a considerable distance. The public right of access to Glen Tilt is preserved as a result of an action brought in 1849 by professional men resident in Aberdeen, Perth and Edinburgh.[123] Scot-Ways has successfully brought actions both to assert rights of way and to defend actions designed to establish that no public right of way exists.[124] Several interested parties may join together in raising or defending proceedings. When an action to assert or to deny the existence of a public right of way has been raised and decided in appropriate proceedings, the decision in the case is binding in subsequent proceedings even upon persons who were not parties to the earlier proceedings.[125] In an action to declare that a public right of way exists it is not necessary to call as defenders the owners of all parts of the route.[126]

Actions concerning public rights of way tend to be expensive and

this may continue to be the case despite the introduction of a procedure in the 2003 Act, section 28(2) whereby summary application
can be made to the sheriff to have it declared whether a path, bridleway or other means of crossing land is, or is not, a right of way by
foot, horseback, pedal cycle or any combination of those.[127] The
expensive nature of such proceedings is largely due to the fact that
there are often debates on issues of a technical character and the
nature of the action lends itself to the calling of many witnesses, often
from far afield. These circumstances, as well as the risk of appeals,
add to the cost or potential cost of the proceedings. The normal rule
in Scots law that the judicial expenses of the successful party will have
to be met by the unsuccessful party must also be considered, which
could amount to a considerable bill especially if proceedings termi-
nate in the Court of Session or the Supreme Court. Even a successful
party may be out of pocket, since he is seldom able to recover the
whole of the legal and other expenses incurred on his behalf. An individual who can show an interest, for example a person affected by
the obstruction of a local public right of way, could perhaps seek the
assistance of the Scottish Legal Aid Board, but there are obstacles to
his doing so where he is really acting on behalf of others. No examples
of legally assisted litigation relating to rights of way have as yet come
to the notice of ScotWays.

    A proprietor or a tenant or other occupier of the land may bring
an action for declarator that his ground is free of an alleged public
right of way. Service on the local authority in the public interest is
normally effected or ordered by the Court. If the proprietor is successful in proceedings for a declarator, the decree is general in its effect
and applies to all and sundry. Instead of bringing such an action, the
proprietor may take proceedings for interdict against those persons
who have been using the alleged public right of way to prevent them
from doing so again. But the interdict will only be granted where it
can be shown that the individuals concerned are likely to use the
route again. If they do so, they are in contempt of court and one
sanction for this is imprisonment. In interdict proceedings the order
of the court will be personal to the individuals named and does not
directly prevent other persons using the route; if they do so, however,
they render themselves liable in turn to interdict.

    The Court of Session in proceedings for declarator has the power, which it has frequently exercised, to lay down the precise line of a public right of way. In doing this, it is normally guided by a 'man of skill' to whom the matter is remitted.[128]

Community councils and public rights of way

Whilst community councils have a limited role in the Scottish planning process, they may play an important informal role in improving communication between members of the public and planning authorities. Community councils can help in their areas to list and record public rights of way and to preserve them as a heritage for future generations. Since footpaths habitually used by the public are likely to be known by persons long resident in the area, members of the community council might usefully interview those people and record their evidence of use, checking in relation to each route whether or not the essential elements for the establishment of a public right of way at common law are fulfilled. The questions they might consider are summarised in Appendix 1 to this guide. A list of rights of way thus ascertained with, if possible, a record on a map should then be sent both to the access or planning officer of the responsible local authority and to ScotWays.

Acknowledgement by the landowner is not a prerequisite for the establishment of a public right of way at common law. Where there is disagreement as to the facts, the community council should refer the case to the appropriate planning officer for further investigation. Aided often by work done by community councils, most planning authorities have compiled records of rights of way and have exhibited maps at civic centres, information offices, and public libraries or have made their records available for the public to see at their planning department offices. Nothing, however, precludes members of the public from taking up the matter directly with the responsible planning authority. In most cases the authority will welcome comment and further information from members of the public.

Maps and rights of way

Ordnance Survey maps relating to England and Wales disclose the existence of those rights of way which have gone through a process of verification and appear on a Definitive List and Statement kept by local authorities. Scotland has no similar procedure, however, and Scottish Ordnance Survey maps contain a disclaimer to the effect that the representation of a road, track or path is no evidence of the existence of a public right of way. It is ScotWays' policy that those rights of way which have been recognised as such in court, or by administrative procedures such as planning approval, should be shown on Ordnance Survey maps, although they represent a small proportion of the total claimed.

Some planning authorities in Scotland have prepared maps indicating what these authorities believe to be the routes of public rights of way within their areas, and ScotWays created and maintains the National Catalogue of Rights of Way (CROW), in partnership with Scottish Natural Heritage. However, these records are not authoritative. The indication of the route of a public right of way in such records does not create the right or confirm its existence. Conversely, the absence of a public right of way from such records does not indicate its non-existence.

Separately, but relatedly, the core paths plans drawn up under the 2003 Act (discussed above) are now suitably mapped and normally available online, albeit they too are not displayed on Ordnance Survey maps. Some core paths will be rights of way, but by no means all. It is ScotWays' policy that core paths should be shown on Ordnance Survey maps to assist the public, thereby helping to achieve the purpose that the Scottish Parliament intended of giving the public suitable access across Scotland. There are provisions for amending core paths plans as circumstances dictate and opportunities arise. The case for including core paths on Ordnance Survey maps is fortified by the fact that they follow clear routes and are not susceptible to non-publicised extinction. Further, owing to the fact that core paths need not be rights of way, such mapping would be in no way definitive about the presence of a right of way, and mapping (or otherwise) could not be used by a party seeking to confirm or deny the existence of a right of way. This would either remove the need for a disclaimer similar to the one needed about rights of way, or make the phrasing of an appropriate disclaimer easier.

The foreshore

The foreshore is the shore between the high and low water marks of ordinary spring tides. Access rights under the 2003 Act extend there. Those are not the only rights that exist there. This is catered for by the terms of section 5(4) of the 2003 Act, which provides that the 2003 Act does not diminish or displace the public rights that relate to the foreshore that are under the guardianship of the Crown. Such rights relate to navigation (including rights to anchor, load and discharge goods, embark and disembark, and take in ballast) and the right of white fishing (including the right to dry nets and catch some shellfish), as further explained in the Access Code at paragraph 2.18. It also seems the public already had a right to recreation,[129] although any argument about that is less important now that the 2003 Act provides for responsible access to the foreshore.

Rivers

Access to rivers has been mentioned occasionally in this guide. Like any right to use the foreshore, traditional rights of navigation continue notwithstanding the over-layering of the 2003 Act. There are public rights of navigation and fishing on rivers that are tidal and navigable. For navigable but non-tidal rivers, the public have a right of navigation in regard to the river and can use the banks for purposes incidental to navigation. Any further use of the water or banks would only be permitted if authorised by some other means, such as responsible access under the 2003 Act.

Other routes

Sections 39 to 42 of the Countryside (Scotland) Act 1967 contain powers for the establishment of routes to enable the public to make extensive journeys on foot, pedal cycle or on horseback, with such routes being wholly or largely off-road. Scottish Natural Heritage is the statutory body invested with the powers to create these long-distance routes. If it decides a route is desirable, it must provide a map of the route and proposals for its maintenance and enjoyment to the Scottish Ministers, but not before it consults with every planning authority on the route. The route may interact with existing rights of way, and if so the nature of those rights of way must be detailed. There is scope for ferries to be included in these routes, and there are powers for the variation of approved proposals.

The 1967 Act also provided for 'public paths'. The relevant sections (30 to 38) were largely repealed by the 2003 Act, but were partially retained (in terms of paragraph 7 of Schedule 2 of the 2003 Act) and continue to have effect to the extent that the rights and facilities afforded to the public under those sections are not secured by the 2003 Act, in relation to land where access rights are not exercisable, and in relation to rights of way. The subsisting powers are complementary to the powers for path agreements and path orders under sections 21 and 22 of the 2003 Act (discussed in chapter 2), but those powers can only be applied to land on which access rights are exercisable.

4
General Issues Around Access to Land in Scotland

This guide has introduced and explained the means by which someone can legitimately be on another person's land without prior permission, and the rights and duties of landowners and others in situations where such access is allowed. This chapter gives an overview of some important considerations that do not fall to be considered alongside those permissive rules. It first explains the implications of being on someone else's land without any automatic authorisation or permission. It then highlights some criminal law rules that relate to access activity and transcend any questions about access under the Land Reform (Scotland) Act 2003 or via a right of way. Finally, it sets out the law that applies in specific situations when someone takes access to land, which, as we shall see, can apply irrespective of how an individual came to be on that land. This is the law that can impose liability on occupiers of land for injury to other people in circumstances that were or should have been controlled by the occupier.

The law of trespass

There is a close relationship between the laws relating to public rights of way and access rights and the law relating to trespass. The word 'trespass' is one that has been known to cause Scots to bristle, and sometimes even assert that there is no law of trespass in Scotland. That is not quite right, but from the other end of the spectrum a landowner putting up a sign saying 'Trespassers Will Be Prosecuted' is likely to be disappointed if it comes to an attempt to do so. The truth is somewhere between the two positions. The reform brought in by the Land Reform (Scotland) Act 2003 has repositioned the truth into friendlier terrain for access advocates, by opening up much of

Scotland to responsible access in a way that is definitively not trespass, although the underlying legal position must be understood. So must criminal law offences that apply in trespass-like situations, some of which actually use the word 'trespass'.

Absent any agreement or quiet tolerance by the owner of the land, and where there is no public right of way or other right of access, the traditional Scots law position is that a landowner can take steps to retain or regain exclusive possession. Considering practicalities, a landowner is sometimes restricted in terms of remedies against a one-time, bare trespasser. By 'bare trespasser' it is meant someone who is simply on land without authorisation, whilst causing no harm or other interference. In civil terms, someone taking unauthorised access to land is liable to a landowner only for actual damage caused. For a prohibition of access relative to a specific individual to carry force of law, a court action must be raised against that individual. As for criminal liability, again this will normally only be engaged in relation to actual damage caused, subject to specific offences relating to access which are outlined below and/or breach of a court order that is in effect relating to access.

In a nineteenth century case, one judge stated that it was 'loose and inaccurate' to say that there is no law of trespass in Scotland.[1] Public rights of way would hardly have been required if there had been no law of trespass. This has recently been considered and confirmed by the Court of Session.[2] It is not loose and inaccurate to say that Scotland's law of trespass is different from the law of trespass in England and Wales; the apparently more lenient approach in Scotland as compared to there may have contributed to any perception there is no law of trespass in Scotland. In England and Wales, a landowner may raise a civil action of damages against a trespasser without proof that his property has been damaged. In Scotland, on the other hand, a trespasser is not exposed to an action of damages arising from the mere fact of being on another person's land. That does not, however, mean he can stay on another person's land indefinitely. Unless he has some other legal right to be on the land (such as a right of way or the statutory rights under the 2003 Act), he must leave the ground if the landowner requests him to do so and, if he refuses to go, the landowner – it would seem – may use reasonable force to eject him.[3] The circumstances where force might be used and how much might be appropriate is considered below, but in general it can be noted that a landowner must not overreact in such a way that might itself be classed as criminal.

The law of trespass – Additional information

The basic position of Scots common law remains consistent with the views stated over 200 years ago: 'every man is proprietor of his grounds, and entitled to the exclusive possession of them, if subject to no servitude. . . . No man can claim a road or passage through another man's property, even for the purpose of going to church, without a servitude, far less for amusement of any kind, however necessary for health. . . . the banks of the river, and even the solum of it, may be private, and may be defended against any encroachment or access whatever.'[4] That being the case, there are various circumstances where the apparently strong right to exclude others is eroded,[5] chief amongst them being the 2003 Act.

That apparently strong starting position rubs against issues of enforcement and a custom of tolerance, which have undoubtedly contributed to the perception that there is no law of trespass in Scotland. There is also the lack of direct criminal consequences for trespass in most circumstances, which is one reason why a sign proclaiming 'Trespassers Will Be Prosecuted' is something of an empty threat by a landowner. (Another reason is that prosecutions in Scotland are almost always by a public prosecutor.) Meanwhile, a landowner may also be disappointed to learn such a sign could fall foul of section 14 of the 2003 Act if it is positioned in a place where access rights can be enjoyed, as it could be characterised as a baseless attempt to dissuade access taking.

All that said, the balance of commentary[6] and judicial authority tends towards the position that Scotland traditionally allows a landowner to exert a significant amount of control over access to his land, albeit there are time, money and other practical implications relating to enforcement.

When faced with someone who is on land with neither permission nor authorisation, a landowner is entitled to raise a court action to recover possession. In the shorter term, a landowner can ask someone to leave and (where a crime is being committed, attempted or threatened) call the police, but the question of how much force can be used to remove someone is a difficult one: much like an access taker who meets irresponsible access or is faced with a blocked route on what she thinks is a right of way must take care not to overreact, so must a landowner faced with a potential trespasser. This is especially the case in circumstances where there is dubiety as to whether the land is accessible under the 2003 Act, as responsible access on such land is not trespass (in terms of section 5(1) of the 2003 Act).

Force may be used if force is offered by a trespasser or if a trespasser is in a dwelling. Other situations will not call for such an instant recourse to force. A landowner should always begin by offering someone a chance to leave of his own accord. Faced with a refusal to do so, subject to the caveat that this should not be taken as authorisation to use force in all circumstances, any force that is used should be limited to the minimum force required; to use any further force than that could be actionable.[7]

The criminal law

Not all activity on another person's land can be justified, whether by the existence of a public right of way, statutory rights of access created in terms of 2003 Act, or otherwise. Some of this activity is so objectionable that it is dealt with to some extent by the criminal law. Important provisions in sections 61 to 71 of the Criminal Justice and Public Order Act 1994 ('the 1994 Act')[8] relate to 'public order, collective trespass or nuisance on land.' The object of Part V of the 1994 Act was made clear by the government of the time, namely to control the activities of new age travellers, field sport saboteurs, and environmental groups protesting about such things as motorway construction. The sections dealing with the removal of trespassers have implications for those using public rights of way and purporting to exercise the statutory rights of access created in the 2003 Act. Section 61 allows the police to act against two or more persons who are trespassing on land with the common purpose of residing there for any period, while sections 68 and 69 allow for similar steps to be taken against an aggravated trespass, which is classified as being on land then doing anything that is intended to have the effect of either intimidating those who are engaged in lawful activities on the land, or obstructing or disrupting those activities.

As to how users of public rights of way and access rights might be treated under the 1994 Act, contemporary guidance from a Scottish Office Circular was to this effect:

> While there may be circumstances in which it could be alleged that hill walkers, etc., are disrupting a lawful activity merely through their presence on land, the Crown Office has indicated that procurators fiscal are likely to confine themselves to taking proceedings against persons who can be said to have acted with the specific and ulterior motive and intention of obstructing or disrupting, or intimidating persons engaged in lawful activities.[9]

There are some specific statutory offences that might be characterised as having connotations of trespass, such as section 56 of the Civic Government (Scotland) Act 1982 (which relates to the setting of fires in a public place) or the Trespass (Scotland) Act 1865 (as amended by the 2003 Act, which makes it an offence to occupy or encamp on any private land without prior permission or to encamp or light a fire on or near any road or enclosed or cultivated land without consent, unless such activities are responsible access within the 2003 Act). Reference can also be made to general criminal law, which would regulate unruly mobbing or some activities that cause an alarm.

There are a number of statutory provisions relating to poaching of birds and animals in terms of the Wildlife and Countryside Act 1981 (as amended by the Wildlife and Natural Environment (Scotland) Act 2011 (asp 6)). There is no statutory right of access to hunt, shoot or fish,[10] and no such right is inherent in a public right of way. On the other hand, a walker or other user of a public right of way or the statutory access rights must not be molested or obstructed in any way by the owner of the land. If this happens, the owner may render himself liable to sanctions under the criminal law.[11]

Appendix 1 of the Access Code contains a useful summary of existing criminal offences created by statute. Such offences might apply only at certain times of the year (such as those relating to non-disturbance of birds during the breeding season) or more generally (such as those relating to trespassing on a railway line).

The criminal law – Additional information

The most relevant sections of the 1994 Act operate as follows. Section 61 permits the senior police officer present at a scene to direct two or more persons reasonably believed to be trespassing on land for the purpose of residing there to leave, provided that he also reasonably believes the occupier has already taken reasonable steps to ask them to do so and that they are (a) causing damage to land or property or behaving inappropriately or (b) have six or more vehicles on the land. For the purposes of this section 'land' excludes buildings other than agricultural buildings and scheduled monuments. Those on public rights of way or purporting to exercise the access rights under the 2003 Act[12] could therefore be trespassers in terms of this legislation.

Sections 68 and 69 deal with disruptive trespassers. Under these sections, the offence of aggravated trespass is committed if a person trespasses on land and does anything which is intended to have the effect of either intimidating those who are engaged in lawful activities on the land, or obstructing or disrupting those activities. A constable has the power to arrest anyone he reasonably suspects is committing an aggravated trespass. These provisions apply equally to those purporting to exercise public rights of way and access rights under the 2003 Act.[13]

Occupiers' liability

Occupiers' liability is a sub-category within a wider category of rules that can impose legal obligations on one person in relation to another person irrespective of whether a prior legal relationship between them exists. These rules operate to impose liability on occupiers of premises (including land where there is no building present) for certain occurrences in an area which they are in a position to control.

The 2003 Act provides that the extent of the duty of care owed by an occupier of land to another person present on the land is not affected by Part 1 of the Act or its operation. This means that an access taker exercising statutory exercise rights is to be treated in exactly the same way as anyone else when assessing whether liability on the part of the landowner or occupier exists for any mishap that occurs with an access taker. Meanwhile, there is case law which suggests an occupier of land traversed by a right of way can be held liable in certain circumstances.

The Occupiers' Liability (Scotland) Act 1960 declares that an occupier's duty towards persons entering the premises in respect of any dangers which are due to the state of the premises, or due to anything done or omitted to be done on the premises and for which the occupier is in law responsible, is to take 'such care as in all the circumstances of the case is reasonable to see that the person will not suffer injury or damage by reason of such danger'.[14]

An occupier's duty of care varies widely depending on the circumstances. The duty is not to ensure the safety of every person on land, but rather to show reasonable care. What is reasonable in all the circumstances will involve a factual inquiry, in which a number of factors will be relevant, including the size and conspicuousness of the danger. Greater or less evident dangers will necessitate a higher degree of care.[15] An occupier will not normally be held responsible for any harm to a person in respect of risks that that person has willingly accepted, which might be the case in ordinary activities like swimming but also more risky activities like rock climbing.

In terms of what this might mean for a right of way, Sheriff Kelbie, after pointing out that it would be ridiculous to suppose that a proprietor would have a duty to make safe all parts, say, of the Lairig Ghru, said: 'That does not mean that it is impossible to imagine an occupier being liable under the Act to the user of a public right of way. . . for some danger caused by an act of his own.'[16] Whilst that approach has been criticised,[17] the safest (legal) course of action for occupiers of land traversed by a right of way (and indeed occupiers of land where access rights are exercisable and likely to be exercised) is to not take any proactive measures that affect the safety of anyone on that land. That is to say, any actions which might cause a danger to anyone on that land should be avoided.

Scottish Natural Heritage has published a useful booklet on the topic: *A Brief Guide to Occupiers' Legal Liabilities in Scotland in relation to Public Outdoor Access*. It can be downloaded from their website at: www.outdooraccess-scotland.scot/Access-management-guidance/visitor-planning.

Occupiers' liability - Additional information

Occupiers' liability is a specialist subset within the law of delict, which in turn can be broadly placed under the heading of the law of involuntary obligations. Only a brief overview can be offered here.[18]

At one time, under the influence of English law, Scots law differentiated between the categories of invitee, licensee and trespasser.[19] The highest duty was towards the invitee, to whom the occupier had the duty of taking reasonable care that the premises were safe, with less stringent duties relating to licensees (limited to a simple warning of any concealed but known danger) and even less stringent duties towards trespassers (merely to refrain from doing intentional harm). It no longer does so, but the circumstances whereby a person comes onto land can still be relevant notwithstanding the abolition of those rigid categories. Thus a higher degree of care will be owed to a young child entering premises for the first time by the invitation of the occupier and known to him to be unaccompanied by an adult than to an individual who enters premises where access is not expected without the occupier's knowledge.

In terms of outdoor activities management, and in line with the observations of Sheriff Kelbie, an occupier cannot be expected to take proactive steps about every conceivable risk. This can be seen in case law where there has been held to be no liability for a failure to erect a fence between a bench and a cliff top[20] or for the non-provision of a handrail at a turn of a man-made path on a hill.[21]

The occupier's duty to take reasonable care applies 'except in so far as he is entitled to and does extend, restrict, modify or exclude by agreement his obligations' to the person entering his property. This allows the occupier to assume a more exacting or a less exacting duty, but this can only be done 'by agreement'. Even if there is an agreement, modification is possible only where the occupier is 'entitled to' modify the duty, which (depending on the circumstances) might be governed by Part 2 of the Unfair Contract Terms Act 1977 or Part 2 of the Consumer Rights Act 2015. These rules extend to notices that are displayed by an occupier. They will regulate any notice purporting to exclude or restrict liability for death or personal injury for breach of the occupier's duty, and other notices not relating to death or injury will only apply in appropriate circumstances.

Other landowner considerations

In addition to the rules relating to occupiers' liability, landowners and land managers should also be aware of certain other rules. The Health and Safety at Work Act 1974 was discussed above in the context of leaving a bull on or near a public right of way (see pages 119–120). The health and safety regime applies to prevent employers or self-employed individuals from managing their undertakings in a way that exposes others to risks to their health and safety. Reference can also be made to the Animals (Scotland) Act 1987 Act, which provides for strict liability for injury or damage caused by animals. This means liability is automatic, even without deliberate or negligent conduct, when the conditions of the statute are met. These rules apply to animals that belong to a species known as being likely to severely injure or kill people or other animals or to materially damage property.

5
What the Public Can Do

This guide goes some way to explaining the wide-ranging rights of access to land that exist in Scotland. These allow everyone to enjoy the great Scottish outdoors, with due regard to landowners and other land users. Members of the public have an important role to play in protecting these rights. Any group or individual with an interest in the countryside can help by reporting to the local planning or access authority any obstruction or threatened loss of a route which might well be a public right of way, or any interference with land covered by the statutory rights of access. Most local authorities and national park authorities now have an access officer to deal with such complaints.

Frequent and continuing use of paths by the public is of major importance in securing their preservation. Paths may be lost by the encroachment of undergrowth or by man-made obstructions. As mentioned earlier in this guide, planning and access authorities are empowered to maintain rights of way, core paths and other routes, but might not be obliged to do so. Local voluntary effort to cut back spreading vegetation before it becomes an obstruction is, therefore, of great importance. Some community councils and voluntary groups take a leading role in organising local maintenance of paths, in liaison with their local access officer.

As to man-made obstructions, the sooner they are reported to the planning and access authority the better. The information sent should be as comprehensive as possible and include a map showing the route and the place of the obstruction (including its national grid reference), as well as the nature of the obstruction, photographs, and the name of the proprietor (if known) and/or any other person responsible for the obstruction (if known). In some cases the information should also be sent to ScotWays, which may be able to give advice and assistance.

ScotWays maintains records of rights of way in Scotland, but it follows from the manner in which these rights are created and extinguished that these records can never be complete. Many of the principal cross-country routes in Scotland are well-established public rights of way and ScotWays has signposted many of these and other routes across the country.

ScotWays' work has largely been done by devoted volunteers, but it can still occasion considerable expenditure. There are many other rights of way that may be lost forever if action to establish or to preserve them is not taken. You can help by joining the Society. Membership is open to all including individuals, recreational groups, businesses, community councils and local authorities. (Local authorities are empowered to pay subscriptions in respect of corporate membership of the Society, under section 13 of the Local Government (Development and Finance) (Scotland) Act 1964.)

The Scottish people have a heritage of access to wild and beautiful countryside. It is up to all of us to preserve that heritage.

Appendix 1
Questions about establishing public rights of way

1. Name, address, email address and telephone number of person answering these questions.
2. Where does the route start? Include all relevant information such as street name, property number/name, town, postcode and grid reference.
3. Where does the route end? Include all relevant information such as street name, property number/name, town, postcode and grid reference.
4. Do you believe the start and finish point to be public places?
5. Do you regard this route as public?
6. Does the route follow a more or less defined line? A photocopy or electronic copy of a map with the route sketched in would be helpful.
7. Do you know who the owners and occupiers of the land the route crosses are? If so, please give their names and addresses.
8. Has the route been used over its whole length by members of the general public as distinct from the owner, and any tenants or staff?
9. When did use of the route by the general public start? Has the public subsequently used the route regularly for a period of at least twenty years?
10. Has the route been used throughout the year and, if so, roughly how often?
11. Has there been any period of disuse?
12. Have the landowners ever taken steps, effective or ineffective, to turn people away from the route? This might include notices or obstructions, such as locked gates.
13. How has the public used the route? Was access by motorised wheeled vehicles, on horseback, by bicycles, or only by pedestrians?
14. Does the route pass through any areas of land that could be classified as sensitive to access, such as a private garden near a house or a field where crops are grown?
15. Please give the names and addresses of other people who use the route or know of its history.

(Signature)   (Date)
_____

NOTE: When completed, please send to:

ScotWays
24 Annandale Street
Edinburgh
EH7 4AN

143

Appendix 2
Introduction to the Scottish Outdoor Access Code

Know the Code before you go

Enjoy Scotland's outdoors. It's a great place that contributes to your quality of life, your health and your awareness and enjoyment of your surroundings. Everyone has the right to be on most land and inland water for recreation, education and for going from place to place providing they act responsibly. These rights and responsibilities are explained in the Scottish Outdoor Access Code.

Know your access rights

Access rights cover many activities, including for example:

- informal activities, such as picnicking, photography and sightseeing;
- active pursuits, including walking, cycling, riding, canoeing and wild camping;
- taking part in recreational and educational events;
- simply going from one place to another.

These access rights don't apply to any kind of motorised activity (unless for disabled access) or to hunting, shooting or fishing.

Access rights can be exercised over most of Scotland, from urban parks and path networks to our hills and forests, and from farmland and field margins to our beaches, lochs and rivers. However, access rights don't apply everywhere, such as in buildings or their immediate surroundings, or in houses or their gardens, or most land in which crops are growing.

Know the Code . . .

Access rights come with responsibilities which are fully explained in the Scottish Outdoor Access Code, though the main thing is to use **common sense**. You need to **take responsibility for your own actions, respect the interests of others and care for the environment – what does all this mean?**

When you're in the outdoors, you need to:

- **Take responsibility for your own actions** – The outdoors is a great place to enjoy but it's also a working environment and has many natural hazards. Make sure you are aware of these and act safely, follow any reasonable advice and respect the needs of other people enjoying or working in the outdoors.
- **Respect people's privacy and peace of mind** – Privacy is important for everyone. Avoid causing alarm to people, especially at night, by keeping a reasonable distance from houses and private gardens, or by using paths or tracks.
- **Help farmers, landowners and others to work safely and effectively** – Keep a safe distance from any work and watch for signs that tell you dangerous activities are being carried out, such as tree felling or crop spraying. You can also help by:

  - leaving gates as you find them;
  - not blocking or obstructing an entrance or track;
  - looking for alternative routes before entering a field containing animals;
  - not feeding animals;
  - using local advice so that you can take account of shooting and stalking;
  - not damaging fences or walls; and by
  - avoiding damage to crops by using paths and tracks, by using the margins of the field, or by going over ground that hasn't been planted.

- **Care for the environment** – Our environment contributes greatly to everyone's quality of life and health. It's important that you:

  - follow any reasonable advice and information;
  - take your litter home;
  - treat places with care, leaving them as you find them;
  - don't recklessly disturb or intentionally damage wildlife or historic places.

- **Keep your dog under proper control** – If you have a dog with you, it's very important that it doesn't worry livestock or alarm others. Don't let it into fields with calves or lambs, and keep it on a short lead or under close control when you're in a field with other animals. If cattle react aggressively to your dog, let go of it immediately and take the safest route out of the field. Take care to ensure that you or your dog don't disturb breeding birds. Pick up your dog's faeces if it defecates in any place where it is likely to cause concern to other people.
- **Take extra care if you are organising a group, an event or running a business** – Consult the full code or our website for information about your responsibilities.

If you're a farmer, landowner or someone else managing the outdoors, you need to think about the needs of people enjoying the outdoors. You need to:

- **Respect access rights** – Access rights extend to most of Scotland so don't unreasonably obstruct people on your land or water. Only lock gates when it's essential for animal health or safety and don't put a fence across a path without putting in a gate to allow access. Providing paths and tracks is a good way of integrating access and land management.
- **Act reasonably when asking people to avoid a particular area whilst you're working** – People respond best to polite and reasonable requests, so keep safety measures in place for the minimum time, tell people about alternative routes and explain why the original route shouldn't be used. Remove information that is not up to date.

- **Work with your local authority and other bodies to help integrate access and land management** – Showing people that they're welcome and working with your local authority, or your national park authority, and others will help you successfully manage access over your land and help care for the environment.

If you're responsible for places where access rights don't apply, such as a farmyard or land surrounding a building, respect rights of way and any customary access, and work with your local authority, or your national park authority, and others to help improve and manage access.

Find out more about your access rights and responsibilities – and also about rights of way and customary access – by picking up the Scottish Outdoor Access Code or visiting www.outdooraccess-scotland.scot. If you are having access problems – get in touch with your local authority or national park authority (see the 'Contacts' page on the Scottish Outdoor Access Code website). If you would like to have a copy of the full Code phone Scottish Natural Heritage on 01738 458545 or email pubs@snh.gov.uk. Look out for other approved guidance which carries the Access Code logo.

Statutory access rights were established by the Land Reform (Scotland) Act 2003 and the Scottish Outdoor Access Code was approved by the Scottish Parliament on 1 July 2004. The rights came into effect on 9 February 2005.

Appendix 3
Questions for determining if you are entitled to take access to land

Where are you?

I think I am on a public right of way.

Rights of way are rarely marked as such on maps in Scotland. A signpost may indicate if it is a right of way. You can contact ScotWays to check their records, and for advice.

You may use a public right of way to travel from one end to the other, or part of the way, using a suitable means of transport. The landowner may not impede your proper use of the right of way. You may not impede others using the right of way (for example, by camping in a way that blocks the route). Ancillary use of the public right of way may not be permitted, unless such use falls within access rights under the Land Reform (Scotland) Act 2003.

I am on the foreshore.

Consider whether you are between the high and low tide marks (and do consider your own safety before getting confused by legal issues).

You may take access over the foreshore and, in some circumstances, also use the foreshore for certain activities (such as drying nets). These rights operate alongside access rights under the Land Reform (Scotland) Act 2003 (discussed below).

I am on a navigable river.

The public has a right of navigation and can also make use of the banks for purposes incidental to navigation. Inland waters can also benefit from access rights under the Land Reform (Scotland) Act 2003 (discussed below), to allow for non-motorised water-based travel or activities.

I am not on a public right of way or the foreshore/a navigable river, am I on land where access rights apply?

Consider the characteristics of the land to determine whether it is 'excluded' from access rights. (There may have been a court case to establish whether land has been excluded. This will normally be binding on other access takers.)

The starting point is that access rights under the Land Reform (Scotland) Act 2003 apply to all land, whether urban or rural, but there are exceptions. If the land is a 'core path' you can be confident the land will not be excluded, unless access has been temporarily suspended in extreme circumstances. Core path status can be checked with your local authority and suspensions must be publicised locally.

Important exclusions apply in relation to any building and its immediately surrounding land (its curtilage), a place of residence and a suitably-sized garden pertaining to it, a school, land where crops are being grown (including for the cultivation of tree seedlings in beds, but not orchards), many sports fields (and always golf putting greens, bowling greens and synthetic pitches), where there are building works or minerals being worked, certain fee-paying attractions, and where access is prohibited by another enactment (such as a railway line).

After considering the above, then consider this yes/no question: **is the land a golf course?**

If so, you may cross the land responsibly but you may not stop to make use of the land for any recreational, educational, or commercial purpose. (Remember putting greens are excluded from access rights at all times.) Please see below for how to cross land responsibly.

If not, you may cross the land and you may stop and make use of the land for recreational, educational and some commercial purposes. The discussion below relating to those activities will apply to you.

I am on land where the Land Reform (Scotland) Act 2003 applies: what can I do?

It is necessary to consider several follow-on questions to ascertain whether your chosen activity is permitted under the access rights conferred by Part 1 of the Land Reform (Scotland) Act 2003 (the '2003 Act').

Is my conduct within the terms of the 2003 Act?

Consider whether you are travelling from one point (A) to another point (B), engaged in leisure or educational activities, or undertaking a commercial endeavour that could double as a hobby.

Access rights allow you to cross land (that is to say, travel from point to point, without unnecessary dallying).

Access rights also allow you to be on land for recreation, education or certain commercial activities. Recreation is not defined: regard must be had to the Scottish Outdoor Access Code, but it seems to include walking, cycling, swimming, kayaking, hang-gliding, pot-holing, horse-riding and wild camping. Education is defined as being something that furthers understanding of natural or cultural heritage. Commercial activity will be permitted where the activity in question can also be undertaken on a non-commercial basis.

These access rights only exist when you are *responsible*.

Is that conduct responsible in terms of the 2003 Act?

Consider whether your actions interfere with **anyone** else and whether your actions are so intrusive to others and to society that they will never be classed as responsible access.

A person is to be presumed to be exercising access rights responsibly if they are exercised so as not to cause unreasonable interference with any of the rights of any other person BUT it can never be presumed to be valid if the conduct is:

- specifically excepted by the 2003 Act;
- is in breach of a local byelaw; or
- interferes with work undertaken by Scottish Natural Heritage to protect the natural heritage of land.

Is my conduct not permissible in terms of the 2003 Act?

This will be the case if you take access:

- for hunting, shooting or fishing
- with an animal that is not under proper control
- to take material away from the land for commercial purposes
- with a motorised vehicle (save where that is to aid mobility for a person who has a disability)
- in breach of a court order or
- for the purposes of committing a crime/breaching a court order.

Are there local byelaws or Scottish Natural Heritage considerations?

Please check locally whether this is the case, including with the relevant local authority or the relevant national park authority. There might be, for example, rules about camping.

Have I caused unreasonable interference?

Assuming you are not caught by any specific exceptions, the answer to this question will be context specific. The rights of others you need to respect include ownership rights, access rights and any other rights. Regard must be had to the Scottish Outdoor Access Code to gauge whether you have caused unreasonable interference.

And finally . . .

My location and/or my conduct means access rights do not or might not apply, what then?

You should seek permission for your activity from the landowner (or a representative thereof). There may be a custom of local access, but the safest action is to discuss your activity in advance or, if proactive contact has not been possible, adapt your activity following any proper request from an owner, occupier, law enforcement officer or indeed another member of the public. If you do not, you may be susceptible to enforcement action, particularly from a landowner. Depending on your location and/or conduct, you may also be susceptible to criminal investigation and ultimately prosecution.

Notes

Abbreviations used in notes

CSIH	Court of Session Inner House
CSOH	Court of Session Outer House
D	Dunlop's Session Cases 1838 to 1861
F	Fraser's Session Cases 1898 to 1905
GWD	Green's Weekly Digest
HL	UK House of Lords
JC	Justiciary Cases
M	Macpherson's Session Cases
Pat App	Paton's House of Lords Appeals 1726 to 1821
R	Rettie's Session Cases 1873 to 1897
S	Shaw's Session Cases 1821 to 1837
SAC	Sheriff Appeal Court
SC	Session Cases
SCLR	Scottish Civil Law Reports
Sh Ct	Sheriff Court
SI	Statutory Instrument
SLT	Scots Law Times
SSI	Scottish Statutory Instrument
UKSC	UK Supreme Court

Chapter 1

1   J. Erskine, *An Institute of the Law of Scotland*, 1st edn (Edinburgh, 1773; reprinted as *Old Studies in Scots Law, vol. 5*, Edinburgh University Press, 2014), II.1.1.
2   George Joseph Bell, *Principles of the Law of Scotland*, 4th edn (Edinburgh, 1839; reprinted as *Old Studies in Scots Law, vol. 1*, Edinburgh University Press, 2010), § 940.
3   *Brown* v *Lee Constructions Ltd* 1977 *SLT (Notes)* 61.
4   The right to remove is however subject to 'an equitable power of the court, in exceptional circumstances, to refuse enforcement of the proprietor's right', as set out in the case of *Anderson* v *Brattisani's* 1978 *SLT (Notes)* 43.
5   Although the 2003 Act received Royal Assent (and therefore became law) on 25 February 2003, Part 1 did not come into force until 9 February 2005, by virtue of the Land Reform (Scotland) Act 2003 (Commencement Order No.3) Order 2005 (SSI 2005/17). (Parts 2 and 3 of the 2003 Act deal with rights of community acquisition and will not be discussed here.)
6   Bell, *Principles of the Law of Scotland*, § 956–958

7   Consider case law such as *Livingstone* v *Earl of Breadalbane* (1791) 3 Pat App 221 at 223 and the recent case of *Scottish Parliamentary Corporate Body* v *The Sovereign Indigenous Peoples of Scotland* [2016] CSOH 65 (particularly paragraphs 31–33), affirmed [2016] CSIH 81.

8   See www.snh.gov.uk.

9   The 2003 Act, section 10(7).

10 The 2003 Act, section 10(8).

11 See www.outdooraccess-scotland.com/The-Act-and-the-Code/Keeping-it-under-review.

12 *Renyana Stahl Anstalt* v *Loch Lomond and the Trossachs National Park Authority* [2018] CSIH 22.

13 *Gloag* v *Perth and Kinross Council* 2007 SCLR 530.

14 *Loch Lomond and Trossachs National Park Authority* v *Renyana Stahl Anstalt* [2017] SAC (Civ) 11; 2017 SLT (Sh Ct) 138 at [31]. That case was appealed and although certain aspects of the Sheriff Appeal Court decision were developed by the Court of Session, they did not disavow the status of the Access Code.

15 Governed by the Local Government (Scotland) Act 1973 and related laws, constituted by the Local Government etc (Scotland) Act 1994.

16 See the National Parks (Scotland) Act 2000 (asp 10) and related secondary legislation for each national park, the two national parks being the Loch Lomond and the Trossachs National Park Authority and the Cairngorms National Park Authority.

17 *Fife Council* v *Nisbet*, Cupar Sheriff Court, November 2009, case reference A149/08. The route was declared to be a right of way in a court action in 1997 (which was appealed up to the Court of Session: *North East Fife DC* v *Nisbet*, 2000 SCLR 413), and an interdict was imposed at that time requiring the Nisbets not to obstruct the right of way or interfere with its use.

18 The 2003 Act, section 14.

19 The 2003 Act, section 15.

20 Douglas J. Cusine and Roderick R. M. Paisley, *Servitudes and Rights of Way* (Edinburgh, W. Green, 1998).

21 (1862) 24 D 975 at 982 per Lord Deas.

22 *McGavin* v *McIntyre* (1874) 1 R 1016 at 1024; *Smith* v *Saxton* 1927 SN 98.

23 (1876) 3 R. 485. See also James Ferguson, *The Law of Roads, Streets, Rights of Way, Bridges and Ferries* (Edinburgh, W. Green, 1904) pages 9 and 67.

24 The Land Registration etc. (Scotland) Act 2012, section 9(1)(d).

25 The Land Registration etc. (Scotland) Act 2012, section 9(1)(e).

26 The Land Registration etc. (Scotland) Act 2012, sections 73(2)(a) and (b) respectively.

Chapter 2

1   *Scottish Parliamentary Corporate Body* v *The Sovereign Indigenous Peoples of Scotland* [2016] CSOH 65 (particularly paragraphs 31–33), affirmed [2016] CSIH 81. This colourful case, which involved campaigners who hoped to camp near the Scottish Parliament until Scotland became independent from the rest of the United Kingdom, is considered in Malcolm M. Combe, 'The Indycamp: Demonstrating access to land and access to justice' (2017) 21 *Edinburgh Law Review* 228.

2   Douglas J. Cusine, 'Access for photography' 2017 *SLT (News)* 21.

3   The idea that photography or filming must be linked to natural or cultural heritage might be because the Access Code (at paragraph 2.9) highlights the examples of 'a commercial writer or photographer writing about or taking photographs of the natural or cultural heritage.' That seems to tie commercial photography only to relevant

educational activities. It will be recalled there is no need for recreational activities to involve natural or cultural heritage. It appears the Access Code conflates two of the purposes that someone can be on land for. Cusine raises this point, and makes the further point that the Access Code's exhortation (at 3.63) that video equipment must be hand-held (a stipulation that is not made in the 2003 Act) does not make sense when one considers that many recreational photographers and videographers will use a tripod.

4   Ancient Monuments and Archaeological Areas Act 1979, section 42.

5   One controversial issue has been the use of surveillance equipment to monitor for wildlife crime. Such a crime, by its very nature, will often occur in remote areas where there are unlikely to be witnesses at the scene, therefore gathering admissible evidence by another means will often be necessary in order to secure a conviction. Some of the issues involved in this are discussed in Phil Glover, 'The Admissibility of Covert Video Data Evidence in Wildlife Crime Proceedings: A "Public Authority" Issue?' 2017 *Juridical Review* 269, but for present purposes all that will be noted is that leaving a static and unattended camera on someone else's land is probably not something that could fall within the 2003 Act.

6   *Tuley* v *The Highland Council* 2007 SLT (Sh Ct) 97, 2009 SLT 616.

7   Malcolm M. Combe, 'Get off that land: non-owner regulation of access to land' 2014 *Juridical Review* 287.

8   Paragraphs 3.38 and 3.58.

9   Paragraph 3.32.

10 Paragraph 3.60.

11 The Swedish Instrument of Government, Chapter 2, Article 15 (Protection of property and the right of public access) provides (amongst other things) that, 'Everyone shall have access to the natural environment in accordance with the right of public access, notwithstanding the above provisions' (where the 'above provisions' regulate expropriation or control of property). This translation is taken from the website of the Swedish Riksdag (www.riksdagen.se/en/documents-and-laws/), from the original Swedish, '*Alla ska ha tillgång till naturen enligt allemansrätten oberoende av vad som föreskrivits ovan.*' Provided the access taker does not fall foul of the Swedish Penal Code, perhaps by causing damage to a building plot or a plantation or other sensitive land, this liberal regime allows a variety of activities to take place on land including picking berries and wildflowers (but not growing trees, grass or certain things growing from trees like acorns or bark).

12 Matti La Mela, 'Property rights in conflict: wild berry-picking and the Nordic tradition of *allemansrätt*' [2014] *Scandinavian Economic History Review* 1. DOI: 10.1080/03585522.2013.876928.

13 *Tuley* v *The Highland Council* 2007 SLT (Sh Ct) 97, 2009 SLT 616.

14 Access Code, paragraph 3.9.

15 Access Code, paragraph 2.7, paragraph 3.9 and part 5, p. 79.

16 *Quinn* v *Cunningham* 1956 SLT 55.

17 Under Section 140 of the 1984 Act and section 189 of the 1988 Act.

18 The Road Traffic Acts are the Road Traffic Offenders Act 1988, the Road Traffic (Consequential Provisions) Act 1988 and the Road Traffic Act 1988, as defined in section 192 of the Road Traffic Act 1988.

19 SI 1983/1168. Those requirements, through a combination or Regulations 3 and 4, are that the vehicle (a) has two or more wheels; (b) is fitted with pedals by means of which it is capable of being propelled; and (c) is fitted with no motor other than an electric motor which (i) has a maximum continuous rated power which does not exceed 250 watts; and (ii) cannot propel the vehicle when it is travelling at more than 15.5 miles per hour.

20 Access Code, paragraph 3.53.

21 Access Code, Part 3, paragraphs 3.53 to 3.56, and Part 5, p. 84.

22 Civic Government (Scotland) Act 1982, section 49.

23 Haddington Sheriff Court, 28 Apr 2006 (case reference B401/05) (available at www.scotcourts.gov.uk/search-judgments/judgment?id=bb0187a6-8980-69d2-b500-ff0000d74aa7). She noted that the suggestion that it was possible for different sections of a golf course to be susceptible to 'A' rights (what she was calling the right to be on land for recreation etc.) as well as for the whole course to be subject to the right of passage 'would subvert the provisions of the Act which clearly intend to exclude persons from being on land which is a golf course for any of the "A" right purposes. To seek to categorise and separate different areas within a golf course would be artificial and contrary to the very specific provisions of the Act excluding all but rights of traverse from a golf course. This is reiterated in the Access Code. To interpret otherwise would indeed be an affront to commonsense and lead to a plethora of disputes/confrontations and likely litigation. Unless specific features exist such as a course being intersected by a public highway for instance, a golf course has to be regarded as a whole and not merely a collection of individual holes, (tee, fairway and green). A wooded area is as much a part of a golf course as a bunker, both being hazards of the game and features of the course.' This observation is highly persuasive but not binding, as it did not form part of the sheriff's ruling.

24 Malcolm M. Combe, 'Access to land and to landownership' (2010) 14 *Edinburgh Law Review* 106.

25 As discussed by John A Lovett, 'Progressive property in action: the Land Reform (Scotland) Act 2003' (2011) 89 *Nebraska Law Review* 739 at 808. That point is perhaps most convincingly illustrated by the case of *Forbes* v *Fife Council* 2009 SLT (Sh Ct) 71, where the overnight closure of a path in Glenrothes (to deal with antisocial behaviour) was sanctioned by a sheriff.

26 Section 7(1).

27 The Land Reform (Scotland) Act 2003 (Modification) Order 2013 (SSI 2013/356), which came into effect on 20 December 2013.

28 [2018] CSIH 22

29 [2018] CSIH 22 (paragraphs 55–56).

30 Consider the remarks of Sheriff Fletcher in *Gloag* v *Perth and Kinross Council* 2007 SCLR 530.

31 [2010] CSIH 79; 2011 SC 94; 2011 SLT 31.

32 The Scottish Legal Complaints Commission had ruled that the complaint was not 'totally without merit' in terms of section 2(4)(a) of the Legal Profession and Legal Aid (Scotland) Act 2007. The Law Society of Scotland successfully appealed to the Court of Session against this decision, which meant that the complaint was then dismissed as being without merit. One of the three judges dissented, which illustrates how finely balanced the case was.

33 The 2003 Act, section 32.

34 In particular, at page 78 it is noted that many cultural heritage sites charge a legitimate entrance fee, but 'in other cases, such as many unsupervised historic or archaeological sites, access rights apply'. See also 3.51, which gives guidance as to how to behave at such sites.

35 Malcolm M. Combe, 'Access exclusions under the Land Reform (Scotland) Act 2003: when does a building stop being a building?' 2017 *SLT (News)* 163.

36 Paragraph 3.18. The Access Code's suggestion that guidance about what curtilage means by gauging what land is being *used* with a building might be questioned, as will be seen in the discussion at note 45 below.

37 Paul Q. Watchman and Kevin Young, 'The meaning of curtilage' 1990 *SLT (News)* 77. See also the case of *Sinclair Lockhart Trustees* v *Central Land Board* 1951 SC 258, where the term is considered by Lord McIntosh (at 264).

38 Section 7(4).

39 Access Code, paragraph 2.11.

40 Douglas J. Cusine, 'Access to gardens' 2017 *SLT (News)* 25.

41 By the Land Reform (Scotland) Act 2003 (Modification) Order 2005 (SSI 2005/65).

42 Countryside and Rights of Way Act 2000, schedule 1, paragraph 3. Paragraph 4 also excludes land used as a park or garden. The English and Welsh regime only applies to certain access land (such as mountain, moor, heath or down, where it has been suitably mapped as that). This means that it covers a smaller geographic proportion of land than Scottish access rights do. It also covers a smaller range of (purely recreational) activities. A detailed comparison is available in Lovett, 'Progressive property in action'.

43 *Gloag*, paragraph 36.

44 Access Code, paragraph 3.16.

45 George L. Gretton and Andrew J. M. Steven, *Property, Trusts and Succession*, 3rd edn (London, Bloomsbury, 2017) at 19.6. In *Gloag*, the Sheriff (at paragraph 36) went on to say of the Access Code that 'such things such as advice not to go too close to a building used as a house and to avoid walking on grass which was closely mown and to avoid disturbing persons working or otherwise using the land does not help with the interpretation of what is sufficient for the purposes set out in section 6.'

46 *Gloag* v *Perth and Kinross Council* 2007 SCLR 530. See further Malcolm M. Combe, 'No place like home: access rights over "gardens"' (2008) 12 *Edinburgh Law Review* 463.

47 *Snowie* v *Stirling Council* 2008 SLT (Sh Ct) 61.

48 *Creelman* v *Argyll and Bute Council* 2009 SLT (Sh Ct) 165.

49 2009 SLT (Sh Ct) 71. And see *Manson* v *Midlothian Council* [2018] SC EDIN 50 (a path in semi-rural Penicuik).

50 *Gloag*, paragraph 45.

51 *Ross* v *Stirling Council*, Stirling Sheriff Court, 23 April 2008. This case does not need considered on its own as it tracks the *Snowie* case. The reason that land was leased to the Rosses (neighbours of the Snowies) was not entirely clear, and Sheriff Cubie (at paragraph 12) highlighted the possibility that this was intended to be a workaround to ensure the land was excluded from access rights notwithstanding the action against the Snowies. By convening the Rosses as parties in another action any such workaround was defeated.

52 *Creelman*, paragraph 66.

53 *Forbes*, finding in fact 44.

54 *Forbes,* paragraph 29. Although measurements for the garden were not provided, the sheriff described the house as 'some distance from the fence'.

55 Lovett, 'Progressive property in action' at 791. And see *Manson* v *Midlothian Council* [2018] SC EDIN 50.

56 The Countryside and Rights of Way Act 2000, schedule 1, paragraph 3 fixes a distance around dwellings situated in access land, giving a 20-metre exclusion zone where access cannot be taken. Paragraph 4 also excludes land used as a park or garden. A detailed comparison of the two regimes is available in Lovett, 'Progressive property in action'.

57 Section 11(2).

58 Section 12(2)(b).

59 Available at www.lochlomond-trossachs.org/things-to-do/camping/campingbyelaws/.

60 Section 12(2)(a), with other provisions about responsibility in sections 2, 3 and 9.

61 Section 12(2)(c).

62 Section 12(7).

63   2009 SLT 616. And see *Kolhe* v *Robertson* [2018] SC ABE 43, where a vehicular right of way was recognised.

64   *Renyana Stahl Anstalt* v *Loch Lomond and the Trossachs National Park Authority* [2018] CSIH 22.

65   *Tuley* v *Highland Council* 2009 SLT 616.

66   *Loch Lomond and Trossachs National Park Authority* v *Renyana Stahl Anstalt* [2017] SAC (Civ) 11; 2017 SLT (Sh Ct) 138, paragraph 53: 'at the very least' the Access Code should be 'taken into account' when assessing a land manager's conduct. This case was appealed to the Court of Session and the higher court clarified certain aspects of the law relating to how to assess (objectively) any restriction of access by a landowner, but the importance of the Access Code was in no way disavowed: *Renyana Stahl Anstalt* v *Loch Lomond and the Trossachs National Park Authority* [2018] CSIH 22.

67   In the case which affirmed the Code's role in responsible land management, the Sheriff Appeal Court saw fit to highlight that the representative of the landowner (who gave evidence) held views which were inconsistent with the Code (and further, that this representative claimed never to have seen the Code and then failed to answer a question as to whether he had given thought to the terms of it): *Loch Lomond and Trossachs National Park Authority* v *Renyana Stahl Anstalt*, paragraph 62. The approach taken in the higher court on appeal – [2018] CSIH 22 – renders such analysis of personal views unnecessary in future cases (as responsible land management will simply be measured objectively, with regard to the Access Code), but the approach remains instructive for the status afforded to the Access Code.

68   *Renyana Stahl Anstalt* v *Loch Lomond and the Trossachs National Park Authority* [2018] CSIH 22, paragraph 63. See also *Loch Lomond and Trossachs National Park Authority* v *Renyana Stahl Anstalt*, paragraph 32.

69   Perhaps as a site of special scientific interest, under Part 2 of the Nature Conservation (Scotland) Act 2004 (asp 6).

70   2009 SLT (Sh Ct) 97.

71   See *Loch Lomond and Trossachs National Park Authority* v *Renyana Stahl Anstalt*, paragraph 14.

72   In fact, it was described in court as 'the antithesis of the *Aviemore* situation': *Loch Lomond and Trossachs National Park Authority* v *Renyana Stahl Anstalt,* paragraph 38.

73   Paragraph 42.

74   *Renyana Stahl Anstalt* v *Loch Lomond and the Trossachs National Park Authority* [2018] CSIH 22 (paragraph 60). For discussion of this case, see Malcolm M. Combe, 'Revisiting access to land under the Land Reform (Scotland) Act 2003' 2018 *SLT (News)* 51.

75   *Renyana Stahl Anstalt* v *Loch Lomond and the Trossachs National Park Authority* [2018] CSIH 22. At the Sheriff Appeal Court stage of the *Loch Lomond* case the court added (at paragraph 64) that where a landowner did have subjective concerns, these might not be enough as to allow for an access restriction to apply at a particular spot if those concerns were so broad as to amount to an argument against access rights in general. This attempt to minimise the effect of subjective views has been rendered unnecessary.

76   Haddington Sheriff Court, 28 Apr 2006 (case reference B401/05) available at www.scotcourts.gov.uk/search-judgments/judgment?id=bb0187a6-8980-69d2-b500-ff0000d74aa7.

77   Section 9(g).

78   *Renyana Stahl Anstalt* v *Loch Lomond and the Trossachs National Park Authority* [2018] CSIH 22, paragraph 64. See further Combe, 'Revisiting access to land under the Land Reform (Scotland) Act 2003' 2018 *SLT (News)* 51 and *Manson* v *Midlothian Council* [2018] SC EDIN 50.

79   See Donna McKenzie Skene and Anne-Michelle Slater, 'Liability and access to the coun-
     tryside: the impact of Part 1 of the Land Reform (Scotland) Act 2003' 2004 *Juridical
     Review* 351.
80   Section 13 of the Countryside and Rights of Way Act 2000 restricts an occupier's
     liability to a person exercising rights under that statute, and specifically notes that no
     duty of care lies in respect of risk arising from natural features of the ground.
81   Section 13(1).
82   *Petition of the Crown Estate Commissioners* [2010] CSOH 70.
83   Such removal or diversion being catered for by section 20(2).
84   Meanwhile, whether the old route of a diverted core path is in fact a right of way would
     be a matter for proof of suitable use for the requisite time in accordance with the law of
     prescription in the usual way: see *B* v *C* [2018] SC FORF 27 (where there was no right of
     way).
85   Land Reform (Scotland) Act 2003 (Path Orders) Regulations 2007 (SSI 2007/163).
86   The need to serve the application on such a person was only introduced by an
     amendment in section 84 of the Land Reform (Scotland) Act 2016 (asp 18).
87   Section 28(5).
88   Paragraphs 6.12–6.16 of the Access Code.
89   Malcolm M. Combe, 'Get off that land: non-owner regulation of access to land' 2014
     Juridical Review 287, 302.
90   Paragraph 29.10 of *The Land of Scotland and the Common Good: The Final Report of the
     Land Reform Review Group* (Scottish Government, 2014) ISBN: 978-1-178412-480-9,
     available at www.scotland.gov.uk/Publications/2014/05/2852.
91   Justice 2 Committee, Stage 1 Report on the Land Reform (Scotland) Bill, paragraph 37
     at archive.scottish.parliament.uk/business/committees/historic/justice2/reports-
     02/j2r02–02-vol01–02.htm. This was the lead committee of the Scottish Parliament for
     the (first) Land Reform (Scotland) Bill, quoting a letter from Scottish Natural Heritage
     dated 13 February 2002 (which noted the inappropriateness of the court system to some
     disputes) and arguing in favour of an access tribunal.
92   Malcolm M. Combe, 'Get off that land: non-owner regulation of access to land' 2014
     Juridical Review 287, 314–318.
93   10th Report, 2015 (Session 4): Stage 1 Report on the Land Reform (Scotland) Bill, SP
     Paper 845, paragraph 399, available at
     www.parliament.scot/parliamentarybusiness/CurrentCommittees/94538.aspx#a51.
94   Malcolm M. Combe, 'Get off that land: non-owner regulation of access to land' 2014
     Juridical Review 287.
95   Under the Civic Government (Scotland) Act 1982, section 56, on obstruction of lawful
     passage, or under the Trespass (Scotland) Act 1865, section 3 and the Civic Government
     (Scotland) Act 1982, section 56, which might come into play if a fire is lit.

Chapter 3

1   *Jenkins* v *Murray* (1866) 4 M 1046 at 1047.
2   1914 SC 633.
3   1995 SLT 507.
4   *Sutherland* v *Thomson* (1876) 3 R. 485, and see now *Kolhe* v *Robertson* [2018] SC ABE 43.
    Kohle v *Robertson* also confirms that parking of vehicles on a right of way is not
    permitted, but acknowledges the possibility of parking at a terminus in some
    circumstances. For roads see Roads (Scotland) Act 1984 Act, section 129(4).
5   John Rankine, *Landownership* 4th ed. (Edinburgh, W. Green, 1909), p. 449.

6   1924 SC 380, at 385.

7   *Malcolm* v *Lloyd* (1886) 13 R 512; *Smith* v *Saxton* 1927 SN 98, 142; 1928 SN 59.

8   *Carstairs* v *Spence* 1924 SC 380 at 385 and 394. The case relates to servitudes but the applicable principle is identical.

9   (1851) 14 D 300.

10 (1866) 4 M 1046.

11 1999 SLT 1456. The case was actually decided in 1931.

12 1999 SLT 1456 at 1456.

13 *Rhins District Committee* v *Cuninghame* 1917 2 SLT 169 at 171 per Lord Sands.

14 *Cumbernauld & Kilsyth D.C.* v *Dollar Land (Cumbernauld) Ltd* 1993 SC (HL) 44.

15 See the Countryside (Scotland) Act 1967, section 78; Civic Government (Scotland) Act 1982, section 133.

16 Ann Faulds, Trudi Craggs and John Saunders, *Scottish Roads Law*, 2nd edn (Edinburgh, Tottel, 2008) at 4.6.

17 [2009] CSIH 13, 2009 SC 277, 2009 SLT 337.

18 The Court has a general power under section 45 of the Court of Session Act 1988.

19 *Mann* v *Brodie* (1885) 12 R (HL) 52 at 57.

20 *Strathclyde (Hyndland) Housing Society Ltd.* v *Cowie* 1983 SLT (Sh Ct) 61 and the *Report of the Scottish Law Commission on the Reform of the Law Relating to Prescription and Limitation of Actions*, Scot. Law Com. No. 15 (1970), paragraph 22.

21 George L. Gretton and Andrew J. M. Steven, *Property, Trusts and Succession* (3rd edition, Bloomsbury, 2017) at 19.18, with reference to the case of *Marquis of Bute* v *McKirdy & McMillan* 1937 SC 93.

22 Gretton and Steven, *Property, Trusts and Succession* at 19.19.

23 [2009] CSIH 13, 2009 SC 277, 2009 SLT 337, particularly paragraph 39.

24 For example, the Feu Disposition of 1951 encountered in *Oliver* v *McLelland or Cameron* (1994) IH, 21 January 1994, available on Lexis ([1994] Lexis Citation 505) and briefly noted in 1994 GWD 8–505.

25 *Mann* v *Brodie* (1885) 12R (HL) 52 above, at 57 per Lord Watson cited in *Wills' Trustees* v *Cairngorm Canoeing and Sailing School Ltd.* 1976 SC (HL) 30 at 168 per Lord Fraser.

26 Cases include: *Ayr Harbour Trustees* v *Oswald* (1883) 10 R (HL) 47; *Oban Town Council* v *Callander and Oban Railway* (1892) 19 R. 912; *Ellice's Trs.* v *Commissioners of the Caledonian Canal* (1904) 6 F 325; *Magistrates of Edinburgh* v *North British Railway Co.* (1904) 6 F 620; and *Kinross-shire C.C.* v *Archibald* (1900) 7 SLT 305. The proposition in the text relates only to rights created or alleged to be created after the company acquired the land.

27 D. Johnston, *Prescription and Limitation*, 2nd edition (Edinburgh, W. Green, 2012) paragraph 19.27. As explained there, it is not wholly satisfactory to justify the potential exclusion of the acquisition of a right of way by prescription over land owned by a statutory undertaker by reference to the fact it would not be competent for such a body to voluntarily grant a public right of way (or indeed a servitude), as that would be *ultra vires* (outwith its powers). This unsatisfactory justification becomes clear when it is considered that a person without legal capacity would be unable to grant a servitude, yet positive prescription could operate in relation to a route on land owned by him.

28 Law Com No. 339 and Scot Law Com No. 234, 2013 at paragraph 5.50.

29 Express provision is usually made for pre-existing rights in the legislation obtained by the statutory authority. See, for example, the Railway Clauses Consolidation (Scotland) Act 1845, sections 39–50.

30 David Johnston *Prescription and Limitation*, 2nd edn (Edinburgh, W. Green, 2012). See also Gretton and Steven, *Property, Trusts and Succession*, particularly paragraphs 19.15–19.27.

31   Douglas J. Cusine and Roderick R. M. Paisley, *Servitudes and Rights of Way* (Edinburgh, W. Green, 1998) particularly chapter 20.

32   Faulds, Craggs and Saunders, *Scottish Roads Law*, 2nd edn (Edinburgh, Tottel, 2008) at 4.4.

33   *Jenkins* v *Murray* (1866) 4 M 1046 at 1047.

34   1937 SC 93 at 132.

35   *Smith* v *Saxton* 1927 SN 98.

36   *Magistrates of Dunblane* v *Arnold-M'Culloch* 1951 SLT (Notes) 19.

37   *Cuthbertson* v *Young* (1851) 14 D. 300 per Lord Medwyn at 308–309. After highlighting a competing perspective, Cusine and Paisley comment favourably on the possibility of a circular route (see note 31 above, at paragraph 20.21).

38   *Cuthbertson* v *Young* (1853) 1 MacQ. 455 per Lord Chancellor Cranworth at 456. Cusine and Paisley record their scepticism of this (see note 31 above, paragraph 20.17), but in the case of *Hamilton* v *Dumfries and Galloway Council (No. 2)* Lord Reed makes this *obiter* comment: 'It is not evident, for example, that a cul de sac cannot be a public right of way' (a remark made whilst critiquing observations made in the unreported case of *Cowie* v *Strathclyde Regional Council* (8 July 1986)).

39   *Cumbernauld & Kilsyth D.C.* v *Dollar Land (Cumbernauld) Ltd* 1993 SC (HL) 44.

40   *Magistrates of Edinburgh* v *N.B. Railway Co.* (1904) 6 F. 620 per Lord Kinnear at 637.

41   *PIK Facilities Ltd* v *Watson's Ayr Park Ltd* 2005 SLT 1041.

42   *Darrie* v *Drummond* (1865) 3M 496 at 501; *Scott* v *Drummond* (1866) 4M. 819; *Duncan* v *Lees* (1871) 9 M 855. Gretton and Steven (*Property, Trusts and Succession* at 19.16) cite *Duncan* v *Lees* as authority for the proposition that a curious natural object, such as a large rock, is not a public place, whereas in *Kolhe* v *Robertson* [2018] SC ABE 43 the sheriff acknowledged that case but still held that a rock formation called 'the forelands' (a rocky tidal area, occasionally submerged and inaccessible to pedestrians at high tide) was a public place (as were a pier and a beach, in this case).

43   *Oswald* v *Laurie* (1828) 5 Murr. 6, per L.C. Adam at 12. In the case of a non-tidal navigable river there is no 'foreshore' to which the public could have resort for purposes of recreation: see *Leith Buchanan* v *Hogg* 1931 SC 204, per Lord President Clyde at 212.

44   2005 SLT 1041.

45   *Love-Lee* v *Cameron of Lochiel* 1991 SCLR 61.

46   *Ayr Burgh Council* v *British Transport Commission (No.1)* 1955 SLT 219.

47   *Scottish Rights of Way and Recreation Society Ltd* v *Macpherson* (1887) 14 R 875 per Lord Justice Clerk Moncrieff at 884, affirmed (1888) 15 R (HL) 68.

48   *Jenkins* v *Murray* above, at 1054, Lord Deas, after remarking that it would be an unreasonable thing to prevent people going to the tops, added: 'I have been familiar with hills myself on which I would have thought it a most invidious thing if I had been prevented from going to the top and down again, and I never knew of anyone being so prevented. But that did not give a right, and could not be pretended to have been done in the exercise of a right.'

49   *Wills' Trustees* v *Cairngorm Canoeing and Sailing School Ltd.* 1976 SC (HL) 30. For the background to this important case, see further Tom Drysdale (ed.) *Making Waves: Clive Freshwater's Memoirs* (Kingussie, Cairngorm Canoeing and Sailing School, 2018).

50   *Mackintosh* v *Moir* (1871) 9 M 574 at 579.

51   *Mackintosh* v *Moir* (1872) 10 M 517 at 519. Sheriff N. M. L. Walker suggested in the *Encyclopaedia of the Laws of Scotland*, Vol. 13, p. 19, note 11, that the idea that a definite track must be shown arose from a misreading of the opinion of Lord President Inglis in the earlier report of that case: *Mackintosh* v *Moir* (1871) 9 M 574 at 575.

52   1917 2 SLT 169 at 170.

53   In *Mann* v *Brodie*, Lord Watson stated (in general terms) that 'the [use] must be of the whole road, as a means of passage from one terminus to the other, and must not be

such as can reasonably be ascribed either to private servitude rights or to the licence of the proprietor.' (1885) 12 R (HL) 52 at 58.

54 *Marquis of Bute* v *McKirdy* 1937 SC93, at 129–130. Similarly, the passage from *Mann* v *Brodie* in the previous endnote continued, 'Then, as regards the amount of [use], that must be just such as might have been reasonably expected if the road in dispute had been an undoubted right of way.' (1885) 12 R (HL) 52 at 58.

55 *Scottish Rights of Way and Recreation Society Ltd.* v *Macpherson* (1888) 15 R (HL) 68; (1887) 14 R 875.

56 *Norrie* v *Magistrates of Kirriemuir* 1945 SC 302.

57 (1866) 4 M 1046 at 1054.

58 (1871) 9 M 574 at 576.

59 (1904) 6 F 620 at 634.

60 1945 SC 302 at 318.

61 See the *Marquis of Bute* case, above, at 129–130; *Cadell* v *Stevenson* (1900) 8 SLT 8; *M'Gregor* v *Crieff Co operative Society Ltd.* 1915 SC (HL) 93 per Lord Dunedin at 103 and Earl Loreburn at 101–102 (a case on servitudes).

62 *Magistrates of Edinburgh* v *North British Railway Co.* (1904) 6 F 620, per Lord Kinnear at 634; *Rome* v *Hope Johnstone* (1884) 11 R 653 per Lord Justice Clerk Moncreiff at 657.

63 2005 SLT 1041.

64 *Mann* v *Brodie* (1884) 11 R 925 at 928. Lord McLaren's judgment was ultimately upheld by the House of Lords. (1885) 12 R (HL) 52.

65 *Burt* v *Barclay* (1861) 24 D 218.

66 *Cumbernauld & Kilsyth D.C.* v *Dollar Land (Cumbernauld) Ltd* 1993 SC (HL) 44.

67 *McInroy* v *Duke of Athole* (1891) 18 R. (HL) 46, per Lord Watson at 48.

68 *Cadell* v *Stevenson* (1900) 8 SLT 8; *Rhins District Committee* v *Cunninghame* 1917 2 SLT 169.

69 *Magistrates of Elgin* v *Robertson and others* (1862) 24 D 30 1, per Lord Wood at 305.

70 *Scottish Rights of Way and Recreation Society* v *Macpherson* (1888) 15 R (HL) 68; (1887) 14 R. 875

71 *Ayr Burgh Council* v *British Transport Commission* 1955 SLT 219.

72 See the *Marquis of Bute* case, above, at 119 and *Rodgers* v *Harvie* (1827) 4 Mur. 25; 5 S 917 (NS 851), affirmed (1828) 3 W. & S. 251, particularly the remarks of Lord Lyndhurst L.C. at 260.

73 2000 SCLR 413.

74 *Mackenzie* v *Bankes* (1868) 6 M 936.

75 See *Smith* v *Saxton* 192/ SN 98, 142; *Crawford* v *Lumsden* 1951 SLT 64 (servitude right of access).

76 *Johnstone* v *Sweeney* 1985 SLT (Sh Ct) 2. This decision has been criticised, but in a way that questions whether it is appropriate for an occupier of land that is traversed by a right of way to be faced with any question of liability at all, even before the issue of obviousness is considered: see John Blackie 'Liability as Occupier to User of a Right of Way' 1994 *SLT (News)* 349.

77 *Kirkpatrick* v *Murray* (1856) 19 D 91; *Hay* v *Earl of Morton's Trs.* (1861) 24 D 116; *Sutherland* v *Thomson* (1876) 3 R. 485; *Lord Donington* v *Mair* (1894) 21 R 829.

78 *Midlothian D.C.* v *MacKenzie* 1985 SLT 36.

79 Countryside (Scotland) Act 1967, section 45.

80 1984 Act, section 57 as amended to date.

81 *Fife Council* v *Nisbet*, Cupar Sheriff Court, November 2009, case reference A149/08.

82 *Lord Donington* v *Mair* (1894) 21 R 829, per Lord Justice Clerk Macdonald at 832.

83 *Midlothian District Council* v *MacKenzie* 1985 SLT 36.

84 See Rankine, *Landownership* 341; *Graham* v *Sharpe* (1823) 2 S 540; *Glasgow and Carlisle Road Trustees* v *White* (1828) 7 S 115; *Macdonald* v *Watson* (1830) 8 S 584; *Kirkpatrick* v

Murray (1856) 19 D. 91; *Stewart Pott & Co.* v *Brown Brothers* (1878) 6 R 35; *Glasgow and Carlisle Road Trustees* v *Tennant* (1854) 16 D 521; *Geils* v *Thompson* (1872) 10 M 327; *Anderson* v *Earl of Morton* (1846) 8 D 1085; *Earl of Morton* v *Anderson* (1846) 8 D 1249.

85   Section 59(3), and cf. 1984 Act, section 87. On the applicability of this provision to the Crown, see *Lord Advocate* v *Dumbarton District Council* 1988 SLT 546. See further 1984 Act, section 146(1); Faulds, Craggs and Saunders, *Scottish Roads Law*, chapter 12.

86   Roads (Scotland) Act 1984, section 91.

87   1984 Act, section 93.

88   1957 JC 1 at 5.

89   Guard Dogs Act 1975, section 1.

90   Health and Safety Executive Agriculture Information Sheet No.17S (rev 1) (2012), Cattle and public access in Scotland.

91   *Lanarkshire Water Board* v *Gilchrist* 1973 SLT (Sh Ct) 58.

92   Civic Government (Scotland) Act 1982, section 49(1).

93   1967 Act, section 44.

94   Health and Safety at Work etc. Act 1974, sections 3(1) and 33(1)(a).

95   Health and Safety Executive Agriculture Information Sheet No.17S (rev 1) (2012), Cattle and public access in Scotland.

96   *Allan* v *MacLachlan* (1900) 2 F. 699; *Edinburgh Corporation* v *North British Railway Co.* (1904) 6 F 620 at 636.

97   *Lang* v *Kerr, Anderson & Co.* (1878) 5 R (HL) 65.

98   *Preston's Trs.* v *Preston* (1860) 22. D 366, a case relating to a servitude right created by implication.

99   *Rodgers* v *Harvie* (1830) 8 S 611; *Preston's Trs.* v *Preston* (1860) 22 D 366.

100 For example, in relation to analogous servitude issues: *Stevenson* v *Biggart* (1867) 3 SLR 184; *Alvis* v *Harrison* 1991 SLT 64. See also *Lord Burton* v *Mackay* 1995 SLT 507.

101 *Milne* v *Inveresk Parish Council* (1899) 2 F 283.

102 1967 Act, section 46(2); cf. 1984 Act, section 64 for the use of appliances to maintain footpaths.

103 1984 Act, section 14.

104 1967 Act, section 46(3).

105 The rules found in Part 3 the 1967 Act have been largely repealed by the 2003 Act but are retained for public rights of way (section 99 and Schedule 2, paragraph 4 and paragraph 7(c)).

106 The *Marquis of Bute* case, above, at 127–128; J. Ferguson, *The Law of Roads and Rights of Way in Scotland* (1904) p. 95.

107 *Macfarlane* v *Morrison* (1865) 4 M 257.

108 *Wills' Trustees* v *Cairngorm Canoeing and Sailing Co.* 1976 SC (HL) 30. A reflection on this important case can be found in Tom Drysdale (ed.), *Making Waves: Clive Freshwater's Memoirs* (Kingussie, Cairngorm Canoeing and Sailing School, 2018).

109 1973 Act, section 14(1)(a).

110 Stopping up orders for roads are governed by sections 68 and 71 of the Roads (Scotland) Act 1984 and the Stopping Up of Roads and Private Access and Redetermination of Public Rights of Passage (Scotland) Regulations 1986 (SI 1986/252) made under section 71 of the 1984 Act.

111 *Macfarlane* v *Morrison* (1865) 4 M 257.

112 [2009] CSIH 13, 2009 SC 277, 2009 SLT 337.

113 The 1984 Act, sections 69 and 70.

114 Opencast Coal Act 1958, section 15, as amended to date.

115 E.g. Civil Aviation Act 1982, section 48; Foot and Mouth Disease Order 1983 (SI 1983/1950) as amended; Civil Contingencies Act 2004.

116 The relevant section of the 1967 Act for country parks (section 48) makes no reference to rights of way.

117 National Parks and Access to the Countryside Act 1949, section 20(2), proviso.

118 Nature Conservation (Scotland) Act 2004, section 20, applying section 20 of the National Parks and Access to the Countryside Act 1949, including the proviso in subsection (2) thereof.

119 Faulds, Craggs and Saunders, *Scottish Roads Law*, 2nd edn (Edinburgh, Tottel, 2008).

120 The documentation relevant to this case (SUO-FIF-002) is available online through the Planning and Environmental Appeals Division, at www.dpea.scotland.gov.uk/CaseDetails.aspx?id=117380&T=20.

121 *Alston* v *Ross* (1895) 23 R 273. See, however, *Hope* v *Landward Committee of the Parish Council of Inveresk* (1906) 8 F 896, where that parish council was held to have no title where the relevant county council had decided not to defend an action.

122 *Alexander* v *Picken* 1946 SLT 91.

123 *Torrie* v *Duke of Atholl* (1852) 1 Macq. 61.

124 Cf. *Macfie* v *Scottish Rights of Way and Recreation Society Ltd.* (1884) 11 R 1094.

125 *Macfie*, above; *Potter* v *Hamilton* (1870) 8 M 1064.

126 *Nairn* v *Speedie* (1899) 1 F 635 per Lord Adam at 638; *Magistrates of Dunblane* v *Arnold-McCulloch* 1951 SLT (Notes) 19.

127 2003 Act, section 28(2).

128 *Mackintosh* v *Moir* (1872) 10 M 517.

129 *Hope* v *Bennewith* (1904) 6 F 1004.

Chapter 4

1 *Wood* v *North British Railway* (1899) 2 F 1 at 2 per Lord Trayner.

2 *Scottish Parliamentary Corporate Body* v *The Sovereign Indigenous Peoples of Scotland* [2016] CSOH 65 (particularly paragraphs 31–33), affirmed [2016] CSIH 81.

3 William Gordon and Scott Wortley, *Scottish Land Law*, vol 1, 3rd edn (Edinburgh, W. Green, 2009).

4 *Livingstone* v *Earl of Breadalbane* (1791) 3 Pat. App. 221 at 222 per the Lord President.

5 Malcolm M. Combe, 'Exclusion erosion – Scots property law and the right to exclude' in Douglas Bain, Roderick R. M. Paisley, Andrew R. C. Simpson and Nikola Tait (eds), *Northern Lights: Essays in Private Law in Memory of Professor David Carey Miller* (Aberdeen University Press, 2018) 102.

6 Consider Lovett, 'Progressive property in action', 760.

7 Consider Kenneth G. C. Reid, *The Law of Property in Scotland* (The Law Society of Scotland / LexisNexis, 1996) paragraph 184 and Gordon and Wortley, *Scottish Land Law*, paragraph 13.09. Consider also the cases of *Bell* v *Shand* (1870) 7 SLR 267 and *Wood* v *North British Railway* (1899) 2 F. 1.

8 See *Neizer* v *Rhodes* 1995 GWD 39–2000. For further detail see Cusine and Paisley, *Servitudes and Rights of Way*, paragraphs 23.12–23.13; Gordon and Wortley, *Scottish Land Law*, paragraph 13–09.

9 HHD 17/1994.

10 2003 Act, section 9(c).

11 Civic Government (Scotland) Act 1982, section 53 (obstruction of passage by pedestrians). This is applied to statutory access rights by the 2003 Act, section 5(7).

12 Criminal Justice and Public Order Act 1994, section 61(4A), was inserted by the 2003 Act, schedule 2, paragraph 11 and relates expressly to access rights.

13 Criminal Justice and Public Order Act 1994, section 68(1A), was inserted by the 2003 Act, schedule 2, paragraph 13, and relates expressly to the 2003 statutory rights.

14 Occupiers' Liability (Scotland) Act 1960, section 2(1).

15 *M'Glone* v *British Railways Board* 1966 SC (HL) 1.

16 *Johnstone* v *Sweeney* 1985 SLT (Sh Ct) 2 at 7.

17 John Blackie, 'Liability as occupier to user of a right of way' 1994 *SLT (News)* 349.

18 In addition to the SNH publication mentioned above, see further the Rt Hon. Lord Eassie and Hector L. MacQueen, *Gloag and Henderson: The Law of Scotland,* 14th edn (Edinburgh, W. Green, 2017) paragraphs 27.04–27.09.

19 *Dumbreck* v *Robert Addie & Sons (Collieries) Ltd* 1929 SC (HL) 51, 1929 SLT 242.

20 *Fegan* v *Highland Regional Council* [2007] CSIH 44, 2007 SLT 651.

21 *Leonard* v *Loch Lomond and the Trossachs National Park Authority* [2014] CSOH 38, affirmed [2015] CSIH 44.

Index of Statutes and Statutory Instruments

Index of Court Cases

General Index